IN CHRIST'S IM...

LEVEL I
TRACK TWO

HUMILITY

TAKEN FROM WRITINGS BY

PASTOR FRANCIS FRANGIPANE

HUMILITY

In Christ's Image Training
125 Robins Square Ct
Robins, IA 52328
Phone: 1-319-395-7617
Fax: 1-319-395-7353
Web: www.ICITC.org

Published by
Arrow Publications Inc.
P.O. Box 10102
Cedar Rapids, IA 52410
Phone: 1-319-395-7833
Fax: 1-319-395-7353
Web: www.ArrowBookstore.com

CONTENTS

Track Two: Humility

Introduction

It is important to approach these manuals in sequence, as each study is built upon the truths found in the preceding manuals. The truths in our first study revealed that our heavenly Father's goal for our lives is conformity to Christ; this course on humility will help us see what areas of our hearts need to change en route to Christlikeness. The next manual on prayer will help empower us to transform ourselves and the world around us. The last manual, on unity, is in many ways the consequence of the previous three.

Our journey with God begins with forgiveness and salvation, but these are not ends in themselves. *God saves us so He can transform us.* Even as we are confessing our sins and accepting God's mercy, we must remember: the new covenant secures not only my forgiveness, but my transformation as well. Yet how can we be transformed if we do not have the capacity to see what we must change? *Humility is the spiritual faculty that enables us to perceive our need.*

Of all virtues, Jesus elevated meekness above the others. He said the humble were "greatest in the kingdom of heaven" (Matt 18:4). What a sublime wonder that, in heaven, the height of greatness is measured by the depth of one's humility. What makes humility such an incomparable attribute? In truth, no other virtue enters our lives except that humility requests it come. Without humility, we might actually be very religious, yet have no sense of attachment to our personal need. Because our sinfulness is masked by a religious facade, we are not compelled toward change or the appropriation of future grace.

Consider Saul of Tarsus (Saul, at his conversion, would later be known as the apostle Paul). Saul had been a Pharisee; he was a zealous, religious man, who considered himself blameless (see Phil 3:6). Yet, on the road to Damascus Saul had an encounter with Christ, the result of which devastated his opinion of himself. Saul's religious veneer, as committed as it appeared, had masked the true condition of his heart. Just as the Lord met Saul on the road to Damascus, so He will, at some point, meet us the road to "de-mask-us." He will expose the vileness of our hearts and remove our masks of self-importance and pride. Beloved, there is no comfortable or easy way that this confrontation with God's Son occurs. Regardless of the manner in which Christ exposes our need, the outcome is that He places our feet upon the path of humility.

Yet, humility not only leads us to possess Christ's other virtues, it is the life essence that sustains and renews them. It is humility that recognizes when virtue is growing cold, and humility that confesses the need for greater faith. Without humility, our virtues harden into lifeless statues within the sanctuary of our hearts. It is humility that sustains the unfolding of true spiritual nobility. It provides increasing wholeness, life and growth to all other virtues.

Thus, when we consider the reality of possessing Christlikeness, we should consider that humility is the path to progress. Every time we humble ourselves, we are advancing; each time we possess meekness, we are embracing sustained transformation. Humility is spiritual progress.

No matter at what stage of *In Christ's Image Training* you are currently engaged, the goal of this course is to gaze deeply into the nature of Jesus Christ. Indeed, as we mature, we will examine many facets of Christ's life, but none are more beautiful to the eyes of heaven than His meekness. He who existed as the very form of God, "humbled Himself" and became man, then humbled Himself further by becoming obedient to death for our sake (see Phil 2:5–8). Of Himself Jesus said, "Learn of me; for I am meek and lowly in heart" (Matt 11:29 KJV). In this section of our studies, we will learn of Him. We will seek that grace that only comes through meekness, that grace that makes room in our hearts for His indwelling.

> In that day you will feel no shame because of all your deeds by which you have rebelled against Me; for then I will remove from your midst your proud, exulting ones, and you will never again be haughty on My holy mountain. But I will leave among you a humble and lowly people, and they will take refuge in the name of the LORD.
> —Zephaniah 3:11–12

Only the humble take refuge in the Lord. Only to the humble does God give grace. Yet, grace is not only unmerited favor, it is His promise to do for us what we cannot do for ourselves. When we confess our sins, when we openly reveal our flaws to Him, when we candidly acknowledge our dependency upon Him, we find the Almighty a ready companion in Whom we can take refuge. We are making progress.

Are we seeking revival? Listen well to His gracious promise:

> For thus says the high and exalted One who lives forever, whose name is Holy, "I dwell on a high and holy place, and also

with the contrite and lowly of spirit in order to revive the spirit of the lowly and to revive the heart of the contrite."

—Isaiah 57:15

God is gloriously enthroned in heaven. Yet, He expands His dwelling to abide also with the "contrite and lowly . . . in order to revive" them. Genuine *spiritual* revival does not come simply because we hang a sign outside our churches and advertise. No, true revival only comes from God and only comes to the humble. How awesome is His great encouragement: He promises to *dwell* with the contrite and lowly.

Beloved, there is nothing God so desires from us more than a humble, believing heart. Listen well to this final great promise of our Creator:

> Thus says the Lord, "Heaven is My throne, and the earth is My footstool. Where then is a house you could build for Me? And where is a place that I may rest? For My hand made all these things, thus all these things came into being," declares the LORD. "But to this one I will look, to him who is humble and contrite of spirit, and who trembles at My word."   —Isaiah 66:1–2

The great King, the Eternal One, sifts the nations in search of a singular type of person: *he who is humble, contrite of spirit, and who trembles at His word.* He says, "To this one I will look." As you humble yourself, as you see and confess your sins, as you ask others for forgiveness where you failed them, the focused attention of God Himself is drawing near to you. He has His power and your destiny with Him.

For years I had this verse, Isaiah 66:1–2, taped to my bathroom window. Each day the Spirit of God assured me that He wasn't looking at my intellect or talents, but my yieldedness. Some of what I have found in the beauty of Christ's humility I have chronicled in this second manual. Many Christians know they are called to a destiny in God, yet Jesus warns that though many are called, few are chosen. Here, in Isaiah 66, He reveals what He's seeking: humility, contriteness of spirit and a heart that trembles at His word. He says, "To this one I will look."

Let's pray: *Lord, I humble myself of my pride and innate tendencies to exalt myself. I long for the secret courts of the Most High and to dwell in the secret place with You. I humble myself before You, O God. Let this day be the beginning of lowliness in me.*

SESSION ONE:

HUMILITY: THE VIRTUE THAT ATTRACTS GOD'S TRANSFORMING GRACE

For thus says the high and exalted One
Who lives forever, whose name is Holy,
"I dwell on a high and holy place,
And also with the contrite and lowly of spirit
In order to revive the spirit of the lowly
And to revive the heart of the contrite."
       —Isaiah 57:15

SESSION ONE AUDIO MESSAGES:

1a. Discovering Your Need
1b. Blessed Are Those Who Mourn

CHAPTER ONE

HUMILITY: THE PATH
TO CHRISTLIKENESS

The bigger I grow in God, the smaller I become.

A CHRISTLIKE MAN IS A HUMBLE MAN

"Learn of me; for I am meek and lowly in heart" (Matt 11:29 KJV). The holiest, most powerful voice that ever spoke described Himself as "meek and lowly in heart." Remember: *Only through the miraculous inworking of God's grace can we become Christlike, and God only gives grace to the humble.*

It is vital we understand that Jesus did not condemn sinners; He condemned hypocrites. A hypocrite is a person who excuses his own sin while condemning the sins of another. He is not merely "two-faced," for even the best of us must work at single-mindedness in all instances. *A hypocrite, therefore, is one who refuses to admit he is, at times, two-faced, thereby pretending a righteousness that he fails to live.*

Indeed, the hypocrite does not discern his hypocrisy, for he cannot perceive flaws within himself. Rarely does he actually deal with the corruption in his heart. Since he seeks no mercy, he has no mercy to give; since he is always under God's judgment, judging is what comes through him.

We cannot remain hypocrites and at the same time find Christlikeness. Therefore, the first step we truly take toward transformation is to admit we are not as Christlike as we would like to appear. This first step is called humility.

In our desire to know God, we must discern this about the Almighty: He resists the proud, but His grace is drawn to the humble. Humility brings grace to our need, and grace alone can change our hearts. *Humility, therefore, is the substructure of transformation. It is the essence of all virtues.*

At some phase in each of our lives, we all will be confronted with the impurities of our hearts. The Holy Spirit reveals our sinfulness, not to condemn us but to establish humility and deepen the knowledge of our personal need for grace. It is at this crossroad that both holy men and hypocrites are bred. Those who become Christlike see their need and fall prostrate before God for deliverance. Those who become hypocrites are those who, in seeing their sin, excuse it and thus remain intact. Though all men must eventually stand at this junction, few are they who embrace the voice of truth; few are they indeed who will walk humbly toward true Christlikeness.

Therefore, sanctification starts not with rules but with the forsaking of pride. Purity begins with our determined refusal to hide from the condition of our hearts. Out of self-discovery comes forth humility, and in meekness true Christlikeness grows.

If we are not enlightened to the depravity of our old nature, we become "Christian Pharisees," hypocrites, full of contempt and self-righteousness. Did not our Master warn of those who, "trusted in themselves that they were righteous, and viewed others with contempt" (Luke 18:9)? Every time we judge another Christian, we do so with an attitude of self-righteousness. Each time we criticize another church, contempt is the motive behind our words. The irony of our Christianity is that so many churches look upon each other with identical attitudes of superiority! *The modern church has become overstocked with those who, thinking they were holy, have become the exact opposite of holiness because they so lack humility!*

Yet the humility we seek is drawn from a well that goes deeper than the awareness of our needs. Even in times of spiritual fullness, we must delight in weakness, knowing all strength is the product of God's grace. The humility we hope to find must go beyond the pattern of living proud lives, interrupted momentarily by intervals of self-abasement. Meekness must become our way of life. Like Jesus, we must delight in becoming "lowly in heart." Like Jesus, His disciples are humble by choice.

ANYONE CAN JUDGE, BUT CAN YOU SAVE?

Hypocrites love to judge; it makes them feel superior. But it shall not be so with you. You must seek earnestly for lowliness of heart. Many zealous but proud Christians have failed to reach Christlikeness because they presumed they were called to judge others.

Jesus Christ did not come to condemn the world but to save the world. Anyone can pass judgment, but can they save? Can they lay down their lives in love, intercession, and faith for the one judged? Can they target an area of need and, rather than criticizing, fast and pray, asking God to supply the very virtue they feel is lacking? And then, can they persevere in love-motivated prayer until that fallen area blooms in godliness? Such is the life Christ commands we follow!

To judge after the flesh requires but one eye and a carnal mind. On the other hand, it takes the loving faithfulness of Christ to redeem and save.

One act of His love revealed through us will do more to warm cold hearts than the sum of all our pompous criticisms. Therefore, grow in love, excel in mercy, and you will have a clearer perception into the essence of holiness, for it is the nature of God, who is love.

One may argue, "But Jesus condemned sin." Yes, and we condemn sin also, but the sin we must condemn first is the sin of judging others, for it obscures our vision from discerning sin in ourselves! (see Matt 7:5) Understand this: *We will never become Christlike by criticizing others; nor is anyone brought nearer to God through finding fault!*

If we are honestly pursuing our sanctification, we will soon discover we have no time for judging others. Indeed, being in need of mercy, we will seek eagerly for opportunities to be merciful to others.

Yes, Scripture tells us that Jesus judged men in certain situations, but His *motive* was always to save. His love was perfectly committed to the one He judged. When our love toward another is such that we can honestly say, like Christ, "I will never desert you, nor will I ever forsake you," (Heb 13:5) our powers of discernment will be likewise perfected; for it is love alone that gives us pure motives in judgment (see 1 John 4:16–17).

Do you still insist on finding fault? Beware, Christ's standard of judgment is high: "He who is without sin among you, let him be the first to throw a stone" (John 8:7). Indeed, speak out against unrighteousness, but be motivated by the love of Jesus. Remember, it is written, "While we were yet sinners, Christ died for us" (Rom 5:8). *In the kingdom of God, unless you are first committed to die for people, you are not permitted to judge them.*

It is also important to note that the ears which listen to gossip or criticism are as guilty as the mouth that speaks it. Do not contribute to such sins. Instead, stop the offender from speaking and entreat him to intercede, as Jesus does, for that person or situation. Your ears are holy, do not let them come into agreement with the accuser of the brethren (see Rev 12:10).

Remember, Christ did not condemn sinners, He condemned hypocrites. He numbered Himself *with* sinners—bearing our sins and sorrows (see Isa 53:12). This is the humility we are seeking. Indeed, the nature of Christ shines brightly through the meek and lowly of heart.

Let's pray: *Lord Jesus, You have set before me a pattern of humility that is breathtaking. As Creator King, You emptied Yourself of Your privileges as God's form and chose the form of a bondservant. How vile and dark my pride appears in contrast to Your brightness. I am humbled by the sight of Your humility. Help me to truly learn of You, that You are "meek and gentle of heart."*

—FROM THE BOOK,
HOLINESS, TRUTH AND THE PRESENCE OF GOD

SELF TEST, CHAPTER ONE

Remember, we are looking for answers that correspond with this training. Please write out your essay answers, allowing the Holy Spirit to provoke your thoughts. You may want to use them for group discussion. Note: we do not provide answers to essay questions. To check your multiple choice answers, see answer key in the next session.

Chapter 1, Essay #1: Why is it impossible to remain hypocrites and find Christlikeness at the same time?

Chapter 1, Essay #2: Explain why it was okay for Jesus to occasionally judge, in certain situations. What was His motive, and when are we permitted to judge?

1. Only through the miraculous in-working of God's grace can we become Christlike, and God only gives _____ to the humble.
    a. money
    b. wisdom
    c. grace
    d. knowledge

2. Since a hypocrite seeks no mercy, he:
    a. can judge others fairly
    b. has no mercy to give
    c. is full of grace
    d. is righteous

3. Humility is the substructure of:
    a. pridefulness
    b. religiosity
    c. weakness
    d. transformation

4. Sanctification starts not with rules but with the forsaking of:
    a. prayer
    b. pride
    c. humility
    d. food

5. Even in times of spiritual fullness, we must delight in _____, knowing all strength is the product of God's grace.
    a. joy
    b. sorrow
    c. weakness
    d. trials

6. Hypocrites love to judge; it makes them feel:
    a. happy
    b. innocent
    c. comfortable
    d. superior

7. We will never become Christlike by:
    a. attending church once a week for one hour
    b. criticizing others
    c. kneeling
    d. just calling ourselves a Christian

8. In the kingdom of God, unless you are first committed to _____, you are not permitted to judge.
    a. hypocrisy
    b. discern
    c. prayer
    d. die for people

QUOTE:

"Meekness must become our way of life. Like Jesus, we must delight in becoming 'lowly in heart.' Like Jesus, His disciples are humble by choice."

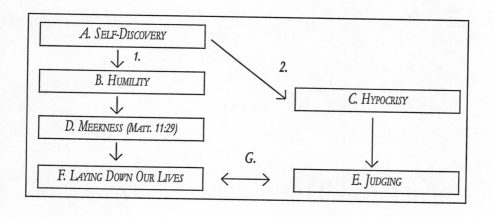

CHAPTER TWO

THE STRONGHOLD
OF THE GODLY

*Satan fears virtue. He is terrified of humility; he hates
it. He sees a humble person and it sends chills down his
back. His hair stands up when Christians kneel down, for
humility is the surrender of the soul to God. The devil
trembles before the meek because in the very areas where he
once had access, there stands the Lord, and Satan is terrified of Jesus Christ.*

WHO TRULY ARE YOU FIGHTING?

You will remember that, at the fall of man in
the Garden of Eden, the judgment of God against
the devil was that he should "eat dust." Remember also that God said of man, "dust thou art" (see
Gen 3:14–19 KJV). The essence of our carnal nature—of all that is carnal in nature—is dust. We
need to see the connection here: Satan feeds upon
our earthly, carnal nature of "dust." Satan dines
on what we withhold from God.

Therefore, we need to recognize that the im-
mediate source of many of our problems and op-
pressions is not demonic but fleshly in nature. We
must contend with the fact that one aspect of our
lives, our flesh nature, will always be targeted by

the devil. These fleshly areas supply Satan with a ready avenue of access to undermine our prayers and neutralize our walk with God.

It is only our exaggerated sense of self-righteousness that prevents us from looking honestly at ourselves. We know *who* is in us, but we must also know *what* is in us if we will be successful in our war against the devil. Therefore, be specific when you submit yourself to God. Do not rationalize your sins and failures. *The sacrifice of Jesus Christ is a perfect shelter of grace enabling all men to look honestly at their needs.* Accordingly, be honest with God. He will not be horrified or shocked by your sins. God loved you without restraint even when sin was rampant within you; how much more will He continue to love you as you seek His grace to be free from iniquity?

Before we launch out in aggressive warfare, we must realize that many of our battles are merely the consequences of our own actions. To war effectively, we must separate what is of the flesh from what is of the devil.

Allow me to give you an example. My wife and I once lived in an area where a beautiful red cardinal kept its nest. Cardinals are very territorial and will fight off intruding cardinals zealously. At that time, we owned a van which had large side mirrors and chrome bumpers. Occasionally, the cardinal would attack the bumpers or mirrors, thinking his reflection was another bird. One day, as I watched the cardinal assail the mirror, I thought, "What a foolish creature; his enemy is merely the reflection of himself." Immediately the Lord spoke to my heart, *"And so also are many of your enemies the reflection of yourself."*

Before we have any strategy for attacking Satan, we must make sure that the real enemy is not our own carnal nature. We must ask ourselves: are the things oppressing us today the harvest of what we planted yesterday?

AGREE WITH THINE ADVERSARY

You will remember that Jesus taught:

Agree with thine adversary quickly, whiles thou art in the way with him; lest at any time the adversary deliver thee to the judge, and the judge deliver thee to the officer, and thou be cast into prison. ·Verily I say unto thee, Thou shalt by no means come out thence, till thou hast paid the uttermost farthing.   —Matthew 5:25–26 KJV

Jesus is speaking here of more than avoiding lawsuits. In fact, He speaks in such a way as to indicate that, in regards to this particular adversary and this particular judge, we will always lose our case and end up in prison.

This parable explains God's view of human righteousness. In the narrative, the adversary is the devil and the Judge is God. Satan, as our adversary, stands as the accuser of the brethren before God, the Judge of all. The truth Christ wants us to see is that when we approach God on the basis of our own righteousness, the adversary will always have legal grounds to "cast [us] into prison," for our righteousness is "as filthy rags" (Isa 64:6 KJV).

When Jesus says, "agree with thine adversary quickly," He does not mean "obey" the devil. He is saying that when Satan accuses you of some sin or flaw, if the devil is even minutely right, it is to your advantage to agree with him about your unrighteousness. If he accuses you of being impure or not loving or praying enough, *he is right.* The key is not to argue with the devil about your own righteousness because, before God, your righteousness *is* unacceptable. No matter how much you defend or justify yourself, you know inwardly that often the accusations of the devil have morsels of truth in them.

Our salvation is not based upon what we do but upon who Jesus becomes to us. Christ Himself is our righteousness. We have been justified by faith; our peace with God comes through our Lord Jesus Christ (see Rom 5:1). When Satan comes against you, he tries to deceive you by focusing your attention upon your own righteousness. The more we recognize that Jesus alone is our righteousness, the less the adversary can assault us in the arena of our failings. When the accuser comes seeking to condemn you for not having enough love, your response should be, "That is true, I do not have enough love. But the Son of God died for *all* my sins, even the sin of imperfect love." Step out from the shadow of satanic assault and stand in the brightness of your Father's love. Submit yourself to God and ask for Christ's love and forgiveness to replace your weak and imperfect love.

When Satan seeks to condemn you for impatience, again your response should be, "Yes, in my flesh I am very impatient. But since I have been born again, *Jesus* is my righteousness and through His blood I am forgiven and cleansed." Turn again to God. Use the accusation as a reminder that you are not standing before a throne of judgment but rather a throne of grace which enables you to boldly draw near to God for help (see Heb 4:16).

A vital key, therefore, to overcoming the devil is humility. To humble yourself is to refuse to defend your image: you *are* corrupt and full of sin in your old nature! Yet, we have a *new* nature which has been created in the likeness of Christ (see Eph 4:24), so we can agree with our adversary about the condition of our flesh!

But do not limit this principle of humbling yourself to only when you are involved in spiritual warfare. This precept is applicable in other situations as well. The strength of humility is that it builds a spiritual defense around your soul, prohibiting strife, competition, and many of life's irritations from stealing your peace.

A wonderful place to practice this is in your family relationships. As a husband, your wife may criticize you for being insensitive. A fleshly response could easily escalate the conversation into a conflict. The alternative is to simply humble yourself and agree with your wife. You probably were insensitive. Then pray together and ask God for a more tender love.

As a wife, perhaps your husband accuses you of not understanding the pressures he has at work. More than likely he is right, you do not know the things he must face. Instead of responding with a counter-charge, humble yourself and agree with him. Pray together, asking God to give you an understanding heart. If we remain humble in heart, we will receive abundant grace from God; Satan will be disarmed on many fronts.

Remember, Satan fears virtue. He is terrified of humility; he hates it because humility is the surrender of the soul to the Lord, and the devil is terrified of Jesus Christ.

Let's pray: *Dear Lord, thank You. You have come to give us life in abundance, and certainly at the core of eternal life is Your meekness. Master, create in me a love for lowliness. I confess my pride, my self-righteousness, my desire to receive glory from men. Unite me with the values of Your heart, that in meekness I could truly represent You! Amen.*

—FROM THE BOOK, THE THREE BATTLEGROUNDS

SELF TEST, CHAPTER TWO

Remember, we are looking for answers that correspond with this training. Please write out your essay answers, allowing the Holy Spirit to provoke your thoughts. You may want to use them for group discussion. Note: we do not provide answers to essay questions. To check your multiple choice answers, see answer key in the next session.

Chapter 2, Essay #1: Why is it that many of our battles are merely the consequence of our own actions?

Chapter 2, Essay #2: Explain why there may be a morsel of truth in some of the adversary's accusations.

1. The devil trembles before the meek because in the very areas where he once had access there stands:
   a. Goliath
   b. David
   c. Jesus
   d. a guardian angel

2. If the devil should "eat dust" (Gen 3:14) and all that is carnal in nature is dust, then Satan can dine on:
   a. our problems
   b. grasshoppers
   c. apples
   d. all that we withhold from God

3. To war effectively, we must separate what is of the _____ from what is of the _____.
   a. army, navy
   b. flesh, devil
   c. enemy, angels
   d. real, fake

4. The truth Christ wants us to see in Matthew 5:25 is that when we approach God on the basis of our own _____, the adversary will always have legal grounds.
   a. accord
   b. mercy
   c. righteousness
   d. grace

5. When Jesus says "agree with thine adversary quickly" (Matt 5:25), He means it is to your advantage to agree with him about your:
   a. unrighteousness
   b. neighbor's sin
   c. perfectionism
   d. self pity

6. Our _____ is not based upon what we do but upon who Jesus becomes to us.
   a. destiny
   b. appearance
   c. salvation
   d. personality

QUOTE:

"Our salvation is not based upon what we do but upon who Jesus becomes to us. Christ Himself is our righteousness. We have been justified by faith; our peace with God comes through our Lord Jesus Christ (see Rom 5:1). When Satan comes against you, he tries to deceive you by focusing your attention upon your own righteousness. The more we recognize that Jesus alone is our righteousness, the less the adversary can assault us in the arena of our failings."

7. To humble yourself is to:
   a. cry out
   b. refuse to defend your image
   c. be a doormat
   d. be wimpy

8. A fleshly response, a counter charge to criticism, can escalate to conflict. Rather, we should:
   a. stay humble
   b. agree with the one who criticized
   c. pray
   d. all the above

SESSION TWO:

THOSE WHOM
GOD CHOOSES

Now the man Moses was very meek, above all the men which were upon the face of the earth.   *—Numbers 12:3 KJV*

Take my yoke upon you, and learn of me; for I am meek and lowly in heart: and ye shall find rest unto your souls.   *—Matthew 11:29 KJV*

SESSION TWO AUDIO MESSAGES:

2a. Blessed Are the Meek
2b. Those Who Hunger

ANSWER KEY TO LAST SESSION'S
SELF TEST QUESTIONS:

CHAPTER ONE. Humility: The Path
to Christlikeness
1.c, 2.b, 3.d, 4.b, 5.c, 6.d, 7.b, 8.d.
CHAPTER TWO. The Stronghold of the Godly
1.c, 2.d, 3.b, 4.c, 5.a, 6.c, 7.b, 8.d.

CHAPTER THREE

CHARACTER
PRECEDES POWER

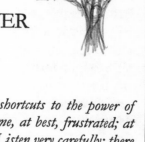

Many Christians look for shortcuts to the power of God. To try shortcuts is to become, at best, frustrated; at worst, a false teacher or prophet. Listen very carefully: there is tremendous power for us in God, but not without holiness. Holiness precedes power.

WHEN JOHN SAW JESUS

Then Jesus arrived from Galilee at the Jordan coming to John, to be baptized by him. But John tried to prevent Him, saying, "I have need to be baptized by You, and do You come to me?" But Jesus answering said to him, "Permit it at this time; for in this way it is fitting for us to fulfill all righteousness." Then he permitted Him. And after being baptized, Jesus went up immediately from the water; and behold, the heavens were opened, and he saw the Spirit of God descending as a dove, and coming upon Him, and behold, a voice out of the heavens, saying, "This is My beloved Son, in whom I am well-pleased."

—Matthew 3:13–17

Let us understand this prophet, John the Baptist. According to the Scriptures, John was filled with the Holy Spirit "while yet in his mother's womb" (see Luke 1:15–17). We are also told his coming was in the spirit and power of Elijah. Historians tell us that John's penetrating, uncompromising ministry led nearly one million people to repentance. Vast multitudes left their cities and towns and went into the wilderness to hear the prophet and be baptized into repentance in preparation for the kingdom of God.

Only Jesus knew the fallen condition of the human heart more perfectly than John. No class of people escaped the Baptist's judgment: soldiers and kings, sinners and religious leaders alike were all brought into the "valley of decision." John's baptism was more than a simple immersion in water. He required a public confession of sins as well as the bringing forth of righteousness (see Matt 3:6, 8).

Jesus testified that John was "more than a prophet." He said, among those born of women, "there has not arisen anyone greater than John" (Matt 11:9–11). John was a "seer prophet," which meant he had open vision into the spirit realm. He testified that he *"beheld* the Spirit descending as a dove out of heaven" (John 1:32–33). He *saw* "the wrath to come" (Matt 3:7). He *witnessed* "the kingdom of God" (Matt 3:2). John had insight into the secrets of men's hearts. His vision penetrated the veneer of the well-respected Pharisees; within their souls he saw a "brood of vipers" (Matt 3:7). Understand this about prophets, they are aware of things that are hidden from other men.

But when Jesus came to be baptized, *before* the heavens opened and the Holy Spirit descended, John saw something that was overwhelming even to his standard of righteousness. He gazed into Jesus' heart and he *saw no sins, no lies, no lusts.* John saw a level of holiness that, without knowing he was gazing at the Messiah, caused him to utter with astonishment, "I have need to be baptized by You" (Matt 3:14).

Jesus, as the "Lamb of God" (John 1:35–36), was without spot or blemish. This is exactly what the prophet beheld in Jesus: *spotless purity of heart.* Christ's virtue took John's breath away! The powerful emanation of Christ's inner purity made John immediately aware of his own need. When John saw Jesus he discovered a level of righteousness that was higher, purer than his own. This great prophet looked into the heart of Jesus and in the brightness of Christ's holiness he cried, "I have need" (Matt 3:14).

And so it is with us. Each time we see Jesus, each successive revelation of Christ's purity makes our need more apparent. As Christ's holiness unfolds before us, we cannot help but echo the same cry of John the Baptist: *"I have need to be baptized by You!"*

Yet, in the beginning of our walk, we embraced life in our own strength, trusting in our own skills for success and attainment. Yes, we turned to God, but mainly in times of grief or trial. But as the Lord brings us into maturity, what we once considered strengths are actually discovered to be more subtle and, therefore, more dangerous weaknesses. Our pride and self-confidence keep us from God's help; the clamor of our many ideas and desires drown the whisper of the still small voice of God. Indeed, in God's eyes, the best of human successes are still "wretched and miserable and poor and blind and naked" (Rev 3:17).

In time, we discover that all true strength, all true effectiveness—yes, our very holiness itself—begins with discovering our need. We grow weaker, less confident in our abilities. As the outer shell of self-righteousness crumbles, *Jesus Himself* becomes God's answer to every man who cries for holiness and power in his walk.

We may think we have spiritual gifts, we may presume we are holy, we may rejoice with human successes, but until we see Christ and abandon our reliance upon our self-righteousness, all we will ever have, at best, is religion.

Oh, let us grasp this truth with both hands, let it never slip from us! *Jesus Himself is our source of holiness!* We are so eager to do something for Him; anything, as long as we do not have to change inside! God does not need what we can do, He wants what we are. He wants to make us a holy people. Let us not be anxious in this process. Allow Him to do the deep inner work of preparation. Jesus lived thirty years of sinless purity before He did one work of power! His goal was not to do some great work but to please the Father with a holy life!

Hear me, our goal, likewise, is not to become powerful but to become holy with Christ's Presence. *God promises to empower that which He first makes holy.* Do you want your Christianity to work? Then seek Jesus Himself as your source and standard of holiness. Do you want to see the power of God in your life? Then seek to know Christ's purity of heart. If we are becoming the people God calls His own, we should be growing in holiness. A mature Christian will be both holy and powerful, but holiness will precede power.

Let's pray: *Lord, I have need to be baptized by You. I see that, if I desire power, I must seek character, for it is the power that works Your nature in me that comes through me as I minister. Continually transform my life, and fill Me with the brightness of Your Holy Presence.*

—FROM THE BOOK,
HOLINESS, TRUTH AND THE PRESENCE OF GOD

SELF TEST, CHAPTER THREE

Remember, we are looking for answers that correspond with this training. Please write out your essay answers, allowing the Holy Spirit to provoke your thoughts. You may want to use them for group discussion. Note: we do not provide answers to essay questions. To check your multiple choice answers, see answer key in the next session.

Chapter 3, Essay #1: John the Baptist was a "seer prophet." What does that mean?

Chapter 3, Essay #2: Why is it a good thing to grow weaker, less confident, in our abilities?

1. Holiness precedes
    a. salvation
    b. baptism
    c. power
    d. repentance

2. John's baptism was more than a simple immersion in water; He required:
    a. public confession of sin
    b. a complicated immersion
    c. the bringing forth of righteousness
    d. both a & c

3. John "saw the wrath to come" (Matt 3:7). He was a:
    a. magician
    b. evangelist
    c. seer prophet
    d. priest

4. The great prophet looked into the heart of Jesus and in the brightness of Christ's holiness and cried:
    a. Lord, have mercy
    b. Oh dear me!
    c. I'm undone
    d. I have need

5. In God's eyes the best of human successes are:
    a. poor and blind
    b. naked
    c. wretched and miserable
    d. all the above

6. As our outer shell of self-righteousness crumbles, ____ ____ becomes God's answer to every man and woman who cry out for holiness and power in their walk.
    a. more knowledge
    b. Jesus Himself
    c. our wisdom
    d. egotism

7. Jesus' goal was not to do some great work, but to:
   a. please the Father with a holy life
   b. have power
   c. walk on water
   d. baptize

8. Our goal is not to become powerful, but to become:
   a. sedentary
   b. weak
   c. holy with Christ's Presence
   d. tired and exhausted

CHAPTER FOUR

PERFECTLY WEAK

As one "educated in all the learning of the Egyptians," during his first forty years Moses had become a "man of power in words and deeds" (Acts 7:22). It is hard to equate this eloquent, Egyptianized Moses with the shepherd who, at eighty years old, was so overwhelmed with his inadequacies that he pleaded with God to choose someone else.

The Lord took a self-assured world leader and reduced him to servanthood. Now God could use him. Having been thoroughly convinced of his unfitness for leadership, Moses was now qualified to lead God's people.

In time, the Lord revealed Himself to Moses, and all Israel as well, as Jehovah-Rapha: "I am the Lord that healeth thee." Yet, God's hands will often wound before they heal. He must cripple our self-confidence before we truly become God-confident. He breaks and empties us of pride, so that we who once were full of self might now be filled with God.

The Lord called Moses to return to Egypt. In response Moses pleaded, "Please, Lord, I have never been eloquent, neither recently nor in time past, nor since Thou hast spoken to Thy servant; for I am slow of speech and slow of tongue" (Exod 4:10).

Never been eloquent? What about Egypt? "Moses the Eloquent" has become "Moses the Stammerer." The sophisticated leader who knew the highest tiers of Egyptian culture no longer exists. This new, simpler man has only one memory of Egypt: failure. God has so humbled His servant that he cannot even remember his days of powerful words and mighty deeds.

For Moses, the very mention of the word "Egypt" floods his mind with weakness; Moses fears returning to the place of his humiliation, especially to lead. Yet, God has not called him to be a leader, but a servant. And, to be a servant, one need not be eloquent, but obedient.

IT WAS GOD'S IDEA

Moses is sure his particular weakness, stammering, will disqualify him. How can a man who cannot speak for himself speak for God? Yet, not only is the Lord unhindered by human weakness, He asks, "Who has made man's mouth? Or who makes him dumb or deaf, or seeing or blind? Is it not I, the Lord?" (Exod 4:11) Amazingly, the Lord not only accommodates Moses' condition, He takes credit for it!

It is a profound thought: God stripped Moses of his worldly place and training, afflicted him with a heavy and slow tongue, and then commanded him to serve Him in this specific area of weakness: speaking!

The Lord could have instantly healed Moses! He could have given him oratory skills greater than what he possessed in Egypt, but He did nothing to cure Moses.

The slow speech is God's idea.

Perhaps we have spent too much time blaming the devil for limitations that actually have their origins in God. What truly matters with the Almighty is not the eloquence of our words, but His power to fulfill them. It's a fitting combination: stammering words backed up with immutable power. "I . . . will be with your mouth" (Exod 4:12). This is the alliance that makes for victory.

Why is the Lord so attracted to the lowly? He knows the weaker His servant, the more genuinely he will give glory to God. So the Lord kept Moses weak and maintained his weakness throughout the wilderness. Forget Hollywood's version of Moses—God never healed the stammer.

Standing before the regalia of Pharaoh's court, a stammering Moses said, "S-s-s-et my pee-e-ple f-f-free!" With the horses and chariots of Pharaoh's army furiously bearing down upon the cornered Hebrews, Moses turned and calmed his terrified countrymen, "St-sta-stand b-by a-and s-s-see t-the s-s-salvation of the L-Lord!"

Who would not be tempted to plead: Hurry Lord—heal his stutter! Yet, the Red Sea parted. God was never troubled by His servant's flawed oratory skills. This is the glory of the cross: self is crucified by it so that Christ may be revealed in power.

The fact is, the Lord seeks those who know their flaws. Paul testifies that "God has chosen the weak things of the world to shame the things which are strong. . . the things that are not, that He might nullify the things that are, that no man should boast before God" (1 Cor 1:27–29).

"That no man should boast before God." Your weaknesses are an asset. God has chosen you, not because of your strength, but because you are weak. Do not excuse yourself from God's calling because you think you are a "nothing." You are making progress, passing everyone who thinks they are something when they are nothing.

Before God, we are all nothing, and we can do nothing of lasting value apart from Him. As

He becomes All in all, we find our place in His glory. It is in our lowliness that God's glory rises to its greatest heights.

Perhaps your last place of service to the Lord seemed completely unanointed. In your mind you feel that you failed God. Yet, it is possible that the Lord has simply been making you perfectly weak. Perhaps it is now time for Christ to reveal Himself as perfectly strong within you.

Let's pray: *Lord Jesus, You only did the things You saw Your Father do; Your strength toward man was because of Your "weakness" toward God. Holy Lord, I renounce reliance upon my own strength. Create in me a heart that depends perpetually upon You.*

—FROM THE *ICIT* WEEKLY MAILER

SELF TEST, CHAPTER FOUR
Remember, we are looking for answers that correspond with this training. Please write out your essay answers, allowing the Holy Spirit to provoke your thoughts. You may want to use them for group discussion. Note: we do not provide answers to essay questions. To check your multiple choice answers, see answer key in the next session.

Chapter 4, Essay #1: Why must God cripple our self-confidence before we become God confident?

Chapter 4, Essay #2: Why is God so attracted to the lowly?

1. In Moses, the Lord took a self-assured world leader and reduced him to:
    a. dust
    b. ashes
    c. servanthood
    d. nothing

2. God's hands will often _____ before they _____.
    a. help, exalt
    b. wound, heal
    c. heal, wound
    d. comfort, discipline

3. To be a servant, one need not be eloquent, but:
   a. beautiful
   b. commanding
   c. argumentative
   d. obedient

4. God commanded Moses to serve Him in Moses'
   specific area of weakness:
   a. leading
   b. speaking
   c. counseling
   d. singing

5. The Lord says, _____ will be with your mouth.
   a. the microphone
   b. "I"
   c. eloquent words
   d. well prepared speeches

6. To the Lord, your weaknesses are an:
   a. asset
   b. abomination
   c. insult
   d. embarrassment

7. It is possible that the Lord has been making you:
   a. strong
   b. perfectly weak
   c. a failure
   d. self-sufficient

> QUOTE:
>
> *"Why is the Lord so attracted to the lowly? He knows the weaker His servant, the more genuinely he will give glory to God."*

MOSES

Before	After
• "educated in all the learning of the Egyptians"	• "overwhelmed with his inadequacies"
• "man of power in words and deeds"	• "thoroughly convinced of his unfitness for leadership"
• "eloquent"	• " 'I am slow of speech and slow of tongue' "
• "self-assured world leader"	• "only one memory of Egypt: failure"
• "sophisticated"	• "stripped . . . of his worldly place and training"
• "highest tiers of Egyptian culture"	

SESSION THREE:

THE ENEMY OF GRACE:

RELIGIOUS PRIDE

But He gives a greater grace. Therefore it says, "God is opposed to the proud, but gives grace to the humble." —James 4:6

CHAPTER FIVE

THE PERIL
OF RELIGIOUS FLESH

TWO TYPES OF KNOWLEDGE

There is a type of knowledge that is doctrinal, theological and instructive, and there is a type of knowledge that is born out of a revelation of God. Both are known as "truth," both produce a certain type of person, and both are accepted as "Christianity."

You can be certain that God wants us to have right doctrines, but we must never content ourselves with merely the accumulation of correct information. For some, Bible study may seem like nothing more than religious facts, where the Word of God is viewed more as a museum than a power plant.

When we halt our spiritual ascent toward God at the plateau of doctrinal knowledge, we become people who never really change. Instead, our old nature simply pretends to be new. The longer we settle for just head knowledge, the more our Christianity begins to degenerate into a religious spirit.

It takes God to change our stubborn, rebellious natures. And our mighty God does not want us to fake our Christianity. He wants us to be real,

Word without spirit.

where the knowledge of our head becomes the reality of our heart. You see, truth, in God's view, is more than doctrines. It is reality.

The difference between mere doctrinal truth and revelation truth is that, with doctrinal truth the heart of a man may be deceitful, lustful and arrogant yet still maintain a theologically true opinion of God.

The Pharisees had, more or less, a theologically true opinion of God, but Jesus said inwardly they were full of "robbery and self-indulgence" (Matt 23:25). Outwardly, they looked holy, but all they had was religious flesh. Inwardly, they were false.

David knew God. He visited the tent of God, where he worshipped and prayed. In fact, even after he sinned with Bathsheba he continued the outer form of his relationship, but his heart was far from God. When he repented, he reverently acknowledged of God, "Thou dost desire truth in the innermost being" (Ps 51:6).

Doctrinal truth has an illusion about itself: the illusion is that knowledge is the same thing as righteousness. It is not. We all know people who are faultfinders, critical and gossips, yet they are capable of maintaining all the proper doctrines about love. When they speak ill of people they do so with boldness, feeling like they are serving God.

What these people have is called "religious flesh." On the other hand, truth that comes by revelation always produces change; it always leaves us less sure of ourselves, more dependent upon God, and more loving toward others.

To topple the old ways of thinking, God must penetrate and remove the arrogance that guards our ignorance. We must be broken of self-confidence and become God-confident. To break us, God must confront us.

The primary way we change is through the Spirit-empowered Word of God. Again, there are two ways to view the Bible: doctrinally or, as it really is, a two-edged sword. When we read the Bible merely on an intellectual level, we may gain knowledge, which is good, but such knowledge by itself still leaves us intact. If we are not convicted, challenged or more perfectly conformed to Christ when we read the Scriptures, it may be because we have a religious spirit that is limiting the penetration of God's Word to our minds.

When the Lord appeared to the apostle John on Patmos, Christ revealed Himself with a "sharp, two-edged sword" coming out His mouth; His eyes were two flames of fire. We need to picture this, for God's Word is a sword. To whatever degree we fail to see it as such, we are probably serving a religious spirit rather than the Holy Spirit.

Consider also Simeon's prophecy to Mary, Jesus' mother. He said, "and a sword will pierce even your own soul—to the end that thoughts from many hearts may be revealed" (Luke 2:35). Notice, He did not say, "and you will learn a lot of handy facts about the Bible so you can win at Bible Trivia." He said that a sword will pierce your heart, and even your thoughts will be revealed.

You see, when we came to Christ, we did not come to a religion, we came to a Person—a Person who knows us as well as He knows His own body. He exposes our hearts: He illuminates those dark, secret areas within us—not to condemn us but to liberate us from the bondages of sin and deception.

You may say, "Well, I need to hear that the Lord loves me." Yes, that is the most life changing, central truth in the Bible. However, Jesus says that those whom He loves, He reproves and disciplines. He then tells us to be zealous and repent (see Rev 3). His love is not on a shelf somewhere, removed from us until we get hurt. No. His love is what motivates His Word as He speaks to our hearts to deliver us.

Consider how the Word describes itself: "The word of God is living and active and sharper than any two-edged sword, and piercing as far as the division of soul and spirit, of both joints and marrow, and able to judge the thoughts and intentions of the heart" (Heb 4:12).

It should be normal for you to be discovering areas God wants to change. It is typical of true Christianity to suddenly see that you have had wrong thoughts or that the intentions of your heart have been carnal. The voice probing into your heart is not the devil; it is God. He wants to set you free from religious flesh.

SUSTAINED BY THE REVELATION OF CHRIST

When God called Abraham, He called him to a promise that was staggering. Although Abraham was old and childless, God told him he was going to be the "father of many nations." Twenty-six years elapsed from Abraham's first encounter with God until his son was born, and throughout the entire process of many ups and downs, the Scripture says, "and Abraham believed God."

Let me make this very clear: Abraham did not merely believe there was a God; no, Abraham believed what God had said, personally, to him. He had an encounter with God's living Word which, like a sword, pierced into his heart. Abraham did not just have a religion about God, he received a promise upon which he built his life.

The faith that saves us is a living response to the Word which God speaks to us. Whatever the Word says about God's kingdom, His power, His grace and ability to change us, we must accept and believe!

Religious flesh is occupied with pretending to be (or look) good. The spiritual soul has its focus upon the greatness of God, believing that what God has promised, He is able also to perform (see Rom 4:21).

Your experience with Christianity will never be sustained by something less than an unfolding relationship with Jesus Christ! The strength of Christianity is Christ! When you are weary, He says, "Come to Me" (see Matt 11:28). When you are hungry, come to Him. Thirsty? Come to Him. For everything we need, He is the way, the truth and the life.

If I don't succeed in inspiring you to draw closer to the Lord, where you hear from Him and are sustained by Him, I have failed in my ministry. Religious flesh is convinced that growth is measured in religious facts. True spirituality, however, is measured in the depth of our hunger for God, where our soul pants "for the living God" like the deer pants after water.

Religious flesh will never inherit the kingdom of God, but a heart set on being real with God will find God's fullness awaiting him.

Let's pray: *Lord, go deep within me. Master, I see that the primary difference between the attitude of the Pharisees and the attitude of Your followers is meekness, and that without meekness, I become a Christian Pharisee. Deliver me, excavate my soul of self-righteous thoughts and attitudes. Deliver me from religious flesh and lead me into the fullness of Your Spirit. In Jesus' name.*

—FROM THE *ICIT* WEEKLY MAILER

SELF TEST, CHAPTER FIVE

Remember, we are looking for answers that correspond with this training. Please write out your essay answers, allowing the Holy Spirit to provoke your thoughts. You may want to use them for group discussion. Note: we do not provide answers to essay questions. To check your multiple choice answers, see answer key in the next session.

Chapter 5, Essay #1: How would you describe "religious flesh"?

Chapter 5, Essay #2: What did Abraham do with the promise God gave him? Please elaborate.

1. For some, Bible study may seem like nothing more than religious facts, where the Word of God is viewed more as a:
    a. storybook than truth
    b. library of knowledge than revelation
    c. novel than a history book
    d. museum than a power plant

2. The difference between mere doctrinal truth and revelation truth is that, with doctrinal truth, the heart of a man may still be:
    a. deceitful
    b. lustful
    c. arrogant
    d. all the above

3. Outwardly the Pharisees looked holy, but all they had was religious flesh. Inwardly, they were:
    a. perfect
    b. false
    c. angelic
    d. both a & c

4. The truth that comes by revelation:
    a. leaves us dependent on God
    b. always produces change
    c. leaves us less sure of ourselves
    d. all the above

5. If we read the Bible and are not convicted or challenged, we may have:
    a. nearsightedness
    b. a real problem on our hands
    c. a religious spirit
    d. a fiery ending

6. When we came to Christ, we did not come to a religion, we came to:
    a. baptism
    b. church
    c. a vision
    d. a Person

7. We must accept and believe whatever the Word says about:
   a. God's power
   b. God's kingdom
   c. God's grace to change us
   d. all the above

8. The strength of Christianity is:
   a. religion
   b. Christ
   c. our denomination
   d. success

QUOTE:

"The faith that saves us is a living response to the Word which God speaks to us. Whatever the Word says about God's kingdom, His power, His grace and ability to change us, we must accept and believe!"

Chapter Six

The Land Beneath Our Feet

As a speaker in citywide and regional prayer conferences, I am often asked to unmask the "spiritual power" opposing the body of Christ in the conference region. City leaders and intercessors have even asked if I knew the "name" of the principle spirit that is resisting the church in their area.

"Do you want to know the name of the most powerful spirit opposing most Christians?" I ask. Eager faces respond affirmatively.

"It's Yahweh."

My questioners, who suddenly look like a tree full of owls, are always bewildered by my answer. They are sure I misunderstood their question. Then, I explain. I remind them that, according to the Scriptures, "God is opposed to the proud, but gives grace to the humble" (James 4:6). So, if we are divided in our hearts from other churches, if we instinctively look down on other Christians or if we are at all self-promoting in attitude, we are walking in pride. As such, the Spirit that stands to resist our endeavors is not demonic; it's God.

The Lord will not excuse our pride just because we sing three hymns on Sunday and consider ourselves "saved." God resisted Lucifer's pride in heaven and He will oppose our pride on earth. What is most sad is, religious pride has been so homogenized into our Christian experience that we don't even perceive it as being wrong. Yet it is without doubt the most offensive blight upon God's people.

The Lord does not want the lost added to churches where they must assimilate the poison of pride at the same table as salvation.

THE ONE WHO SEEKS AND JUDGES

Jesus said of Himself, "I do not seek My glory." Yet, how many of our actions are expended doing the exact opposite of the nature of Christ! Our choice of clothes and cars, homes and roles in life so often have self-exaltation working in the background. Jesus continued, "there is One who seeks and judges" (John 8:50). Listen carefully to His words, for every time we seek to exalt ourselves we run face to face with God. One dimension of the Father's heart is that He "seeks [glory] and judges" those who, through pride, exalt themselves. Indeed, my friends, consider with godly fear our American tradition of self-promotion. Though it is highly esteemed among men, it is actually "detestable in the sight of God" (Luke 16:15).

The Old Testament is replete with examples documenting the Almighty's opposition to man's pride. Time after time it was not Israel's enemies that thwarted national prosperity, it was God. From generation to generation, the Lord allowed Israel's adversaries to humble His people, to drive them toward desperation, humility and finally repentance. There, in brokenness and honesty, God could deal with their sins and finally lead them into national revival.

Listen how the Lord pleaded with Israel: "Oh, that My people would listen to Me, that Israel would walk in My ways! I would quickly subdue their enemies, and turn My hand against their adversaries" (Ps 81:13–14).

So also with us. We need the might of God to be unleashed against our foes. For truly, terrible powers of darkness have invaded our land, and our adversary stalks our streets seeking whom he may devour. Our hope, however, is not merely in confronting the enemy, but in allowing God to confront us. Our victory over the enemy is directly attached to our full surrender to God.

If we truly learned of Him, we too would be "meek and lowly in heart" (Matt 11:29 KJV). And God, who gives grace to the humble, would rescue us from the spiritual enemies of our nation.

HEAL OUR LAND

The promise of the Lord is familiar. He says, "If My people who are called by My name humble themselves and pray, and seek My face and turn from their wicked ways, then I will hear from heaven, will forgive their sin, and will heal their land" (2 Chron 7:14). You say, But I'm humbling myself and praying. Yes, but our humility to God is not complete until we learn to humble ourselves to one another.

The fact is, because of pride, we have yet to accept what the Lord means in His words, "If My people." We still interpret His phrase "My people" to mean "our people"—our limited circle of friends, relatives and Christians whose culture or style of worship is, more or less, like our own.

However, when the Lord thinks of His people, He sees a more expansive group. He includes all who have been born again in a city. All of us who "are called by [His] name," though we are diverse in gifts and assignments, must find unity of spirit before Him. And this begins with an amazing strategy: we must humble ourselves.

I know this goes against the grain of our historic church relationships. Satan has not only divided us from others, he has made us proud that we are separate. We think being separate is a virtue. But consider: only one group of people consistently found the Lord confronting and resisting them in the New Testament: the Pharisees. Literally translated, the word "Pharisee" meant "the separate." Of all the religious groups in the first century, it is the pride of the Pharisees that, today, the church most resembles.

We pray, "Lord, heal our land." But the land He intends to heal first is that which exists beneath the feet of the humble. It is the world of the praying meek, who find the transforming power of God as their companion.

The Lord's remedy for our society is hidden within the life-relationships of Christians. We are always so mindful of what others have done wrong to us, but where have we failed others? What can we do to heal the land that exists between us and those whom we have hurt?

You see, as we become those who "humble themselves and pray" about what we have done wrong, healing from God begins to flow. When white Christians humble themselves and ask for forgiveness from African and Native Americans, God begins to heal the land under their feet.

If God resists the proud, remember also, He gives grace to the humble. Grace is more than being covered; it is being cleansed and changed by the power of God. Grace is God's transforming power doing in us what we cannot do for ourselves.

When we pray, "heal our land," it is the land beneath the feet of the humble that God promises to touch and restore to blessedness.

Let's pray: *Dear Father, You said the healing of our land begins with the humbling of ourselves. Master, reveal to my heart those with whom I am estranged. Grant me courage to forgive and honesty to see where I contributed to the strife. I long to be an ambassador of reconciliation. Therefore, lead me to bring healing to the relationships in our world, and so bring healing to the land in which I dwell. In Jesus' name. Amen.*

—FROM THE *ICIT* WEEKLY MAILER

SELF TEST, CHAPTER SIX

Remember, we are looking for answers that correspond with this training. Please write out your essay answers, allowing the Holy Spirit to provoke your thoughts. You may want to use them for group discussion. Note: we do not provide answers to essay questions. To check your multiple choice answers, see answer key in the next session.

Chapter 6, Essay #1: How does God react to self-promotion?

Chapter 6, Essay #2: What land does God intend to heal first? Why?

1. God is opposed to the _____, but gives grace to the _____ (James 4:6).
    a. wealthy, poor
    b. proud, humble
    c. young, old
    d. strong, weak

2. The spirit that stands to resist our striving for success may not be demonic; it may be:
    a. our in-law's
    b. Abraham's
    c. God's
    d. Zeus'

3. The Lord does not want the lost added to churches where they must accept salvation mixed with:
    a. having to sing hymns
    b. a ruling church board
    c. off-street parking
    d. the poison of pride

4. One dimension of the Father's heart is that He:
   a. seeks glory
   b. has no mercy
   c. judges pride
   d. both a & c

5. Our victory over the enemy is directly attached to our:
   a. aim
   b. strategy
   c. full surrender to God
   d. cell group size

6. Our humility to God is not complete until we learn to humble ourselves to:
   a. idols
   b. one another
   c. those bigger than us
   d. a golden calf

7. Literally translated, the word "Pharisee" meant:
   a. a religious person
   b. hypocrite
   c. the separate
   d. untruth

8. God will begin to heal the land under our feet when there is repentance and forgiveness between:
   a. Whites and African Americans
   b. each race, creed and color
   c. Native Americans and those from European backgrounds
   d. all the above

QUOTE:

"We pray, 'Lord, heal our land.' But the land He intends to heal first is that which exists beneath the feet of the humble. It is the world of the praying meek, who find the transforming power of God as their companion."

Session Four:

The Sacrifices of God: A Broken and Contrite Heart

For Thou dost not delight in sacrifice, otherwise I would give it; Thou art not pleased with burnt offering. The sacrifices of God are a broken spirit; A broken and a contrite heart, O God, Thou wilt not despise.

—*Psalm 51:16–17*

Luke 20
Matt 13

CHAPTER SEVEN

BROKENNESS CREATES OPENNESS

Up until the moment Christ enters our lives, surrounding our souls there exists a hard outer shell, a "survival nature," which protects us against life's harshest offenses. This shell is necessary while we are in the world, but becomes an enemy to our new life in Christ, where the nature of Christ becomes our shelter. Thus, as the shell of a seed, a nut or an egg must be broken before its inner life comes forth, so it is with us: the "shell" of our outer nature must also break in order to free the Spirit of Christ to arise in our hearts.

This need to be broken is recorded in Luke 20. Jesus Christ described Himself as the very cornerstone and source of life itself. Yet, as such, He also said that He was, "The stone which the builders rejected" (v 17). Even though we say we believe in Him, yet how often we reject the wisdom of His words when we build our lives! This self-sufficiency and self will is what must break before we can ever fulfill the will of God, which is Christlikeness. It is only because we are still unbroken that we trust the ways of men rather than God.

areas of life

Proverbs

Yet, Jesus warned, "Everyone who falls on that stone will be broken to pieces; but on whomever it falls, it will scatter him like dust" (Luke 20:18). He is saying that, ultimately, only two types of people will remain: the broken and those scattered like dust. Only the broken can survive the coming glory of God. We either fall and break on Christ or He will fall upon us and scatter us like dust.

God brings low those He plans to use. Consider our spiritual heroes: Joseph, Moses, David. Each suffered an extended time of wounding and breaking until they became low enough for God to raise them up. Or consider the early disciples: they enjoyed limited success working with Jesus, but in His most crucial hour they all failed Him. Even the inner circle of Peter, James and John failed the Lord. They slept at a time when Jesus desperately needed their prayer and companionship. In cowardice, they denied they ever knew Him. Yet, their failure did not disqualify them. Amazingly, because God used their failure to produce humility, they received qualifying grace. On Pentecost, God raised them up in power to represent the risen Christ!

Failure functionalizes our capacity to live more perfectly dependent on Christ. It causes us to more genuinely rely upon the Lord for wisdom, virtue and strength. It cripples our strength, turning the heart away from itself. We learn to fall upon Christ and, though broken to pieces, the Son of God can now flow out through us to others.

Sin is not our worst enemy; worse than sin is "self." Thus, as a hammer is to the shell of a walnut, so are our mistakes in the hands of our Heavenly Father; God uses them to unlock our spiritual inner nature. On the other hand, if we do not bring our failures to God in humility and repentance, they actually cause the opposite effect: they can create a thicker outer hardness. We may become cynical and angry, blaming others for our difficulties. If we do not see the Lord orchestrating our circumstances, we become entombed in our humanity, never able to see the true life of Christ emerge through us.

Let me also clarify that Jesus said that He would not break "a bruised reed." For those who come to Him devastated by tragedy, Jesus immediately seeks to bring healing. God's goal in all things is to create within us dependency upon Him. We either come with brokenness or He will supply it.

WHEAT AND TARES

Another means of breaking comes in how we deal with offenses. We live in an imperfect world for a reason: God seeks to perfect character here. In Matthew 13, Jesus explained that two types of people grow side by side in the kingdom: one He called "wheat" and the other "tares." He sowed wheat, but an enemy came later and sowed tares. Until the harvest, the appearance of tares is quite similar to wheat. Thus, when asked if the tares should be uprooted, the farmer (Jesus) said, "No; lest while you are gathering up the tares, you may root up the wheat with them. Allow both to grow together until the harvest" (vv 29–30).

Why will Jesus let wheat and tares grow side by side? Tares *perfect the character of the wheat*. Why wait until the harvest? Because it is only then that the difference between wheat and tares becomes evident. At harvest, the wheat head, full of mature grain, bows, while the tares remain stiff and unbending. The contrast is plain: the bowed versus the unbowed; the humble versus the stiff-necked.

This parable also tells us that we have no right to judge, uproot or even try to "discern" the tares before the harvest time; even Jesus will not remove them until then. The question we need to ask is

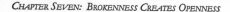

not, "Who is a tare?" but "Am I truly a wheat?" Remember, prior to the harvest, the differences, outwardly, are indistinguishable. In fact, both survive the storms, droughts and blights that strike each equally. Yet, one produces grain, while the other is barren; one becomes valuable, while the other is gathered to be burned.

God allows the tares to grow side by side with the wheat to perfect Christlikeness in the wheat. When offended, the wheat humbly forgives; when faced with conflict or failure, the wheat does not blame others. In fact, the wheat does not even judge the tares, it prays for them. That's how you know you are a wheat. On the other hand, the tares cannot deal with the imperfections of the wheat; they judge the wheat, and other tares as well. They become angry, bitter at life and easily offended. They are the unbroken. You know you are becoming a tare if, instead of interceding for the imperfections of people around you, you simply criticize them. If you carry offenses from years ago and still blame people for your failure, you are avoiding the wheat, you are becoming a tare. At its essence, the difference between the wheat and tares is the measure of love functioning in each; the wheat is able to truly bow to its Creator.

Let's pray: *Lord Jesus, I see and abhor my old nature. I shun the prison of a hardened heart. I choose to fall upon You. May I remain broken so You don't have to break me. May I minister to the tares as You did as a Friend of sinners.*

—FROM THE *ICIT* WEEKLY MAILER

SELF TEST, CHAPTER SEVEN

Remember, we are looking for answers that correspond with this training. Please write out your essay answers, allowing the Holy Spirit to provoke your thoughts. You may want to use them for group discussion. Note: we do not provide answers to essay questions. To check your multiple choice answers, see answer key in the next session.

Chapter 7, Essay #1: How does failure help us to succeed?

Chapter 7, Essay #2: How can we know if we are becoming tares?

1. In order for Christ to arise in our hearts and to free the Spirit of Christ in us, the "shell" of our outer nature must:
   a. become thicker
   b. be broken
   c. not crack under pressure
   d. become impenetrable

2. It is only because we are still unbroken that we trust the ways of:
   a. God and not men
   b. the Zodiac, not Jesus
   c. men, not God
   d. survival, not the Lord

3. God brings _____ those He plans to use.
   a. blessings to
   b. to higher ground
   c. low
   d. much sorrow to

4. Once we are broken, the Son of God can:
   a. never use us again
   b. put us back together again
   c. flow out through us to others
   d. tell us our ministries are over

5. Sin is not our worst enemy; our worst enemy is:
   a. time
   b. procrastination
   c. pleasure
   d. self

6. God's goal in all things is to create within us:
   a. dependency on Him alone
   b. needs
   c. wounds
   d. cynicism

7. Tares _____ the character of the wheat.
   a. choke out
   b. destroy
   c. perfect
   d. uproot

8. The wheat:
   a. does not blame others
   b. humbly forgives
   c. prays for the tares
   d. all the above

CHAPTER EIGHT

THE UNSHRUNK CLOTH

Just as our failures can break us, so God allows other situations to reduce us. I know, we think
of ministry in terms of wholeness and expansion,
but much of what is seen outwardly is attached to
the work of God inwardly. In fact, one way we
expand is to be willing to shrink. What do I mean?
Listen to what Jesus taught:

> No one sews a patch of unshrunk cloth
> on an old garment; otherwise the patch
> pulls away from it, the new from the old,
> and a worse tear results.   —Mark 2:21

The Lord says that you cannot mend an old
garment with a new patch because once the garment is washed the patch will begin to shrink. As
a result, it will pull away from the garment and a
worse tear occurs. I have seen it happen in many
churches: someone is brought in to fix a situation,
but they understand "ministry" as being an opportunity to display what they can do; they have yet
to be cut to size. As a result, when they see the
little hole God wants them to fill, as they reluc-
tantly shrink, they pull away from the old garment,
causing a worse tear than at first.

So, a wise seamstress will soak a new patch in
hot water before sewing it onto the older garment.
This gives time for the patch to shrink to the size

that is needed. After it is shrunk, she then sews it permanently into the old garment.

The Lord must also shrink us before He can use us. When we come to a church or join a ministry team, we cannot help but be aware of the dozens of things we feel qualified to accomplish. In fact, we look at others and think, "I could do better than that." If you are looking at the assignment someone else has and feel you could do better, it is because you are still, to some degree, unshrunk. God hasn't brought you into the body to do someone else's task; He wants you to focus upon your own, even if it is seemingly insignificant.

We argue, "But how will I advance unless someone sees my talents?" The Lord said, "He who is faithful in a very little thing is faithful also in much" (Luke 16:10). We must simply do the thing God tells us and not envy others and their tasks. We seek to do some great thing for God; but God wants us to do little things as though they were great. The entire ministry does not need repair, just the hole we are called to fill. Each ministry has an exact size requirement.

How does the Lord reduce you so you can be useful? Like the seamstress, He puts you in hot water. God must shrink us from our exaggerated opinion of ourselves before He can use us in greater projects. We must simply fill the size of the need before us without envying the tasks of others. If you find yourself, for a time, in hot water, it might be because you took on tasks that were beyond the Lord's assignment for you. He is shrinking you to the size of your calling.

The end of it all is this: the Lord takes seriously His plan for our lives. He has one goal with us: create us in the image of Christ. In His wonderful, all-powerful hands, He can use our failures, "tare-able" people, and our time in hot water to work for both our good and His glory in our lives.

Let's pray: *Lord, shrink me to the right size for the task at hand. May I cover the need without ambition to be seen. Uproot hidden jealousies within me, lest I find myself striving to take the place of others. Amen.*

—FROM THE *ICIT* WEEKLY MAILER

SELF TEST, CHAPTER EIGHT

Remember, we are looking for answers that correspond with this training. Please write out your essay answers, allowing the Holy Spirit to provoke your thoughts. You may want to use them for group discussion. Note: we do not provide answers to essay questions. To check your multiple choice answers, see answer key in the next session.

Chapter 8, Essay #1: Why must an old cloth be shrunk before it is sewn to a new cloth?

1. Just as our failures break us, so God allows other situations to:
    a. hurt us
    b. exalt us
    c. reduce us
    d. make us happy

2. Cloth must be _____ so that it does not pull away and tear.
    a. dyed
    b. shrunk
    c. anointed
    d. prayed over

3. If we are looking at the assignment someone else has and feel we could do better, it may be because we:
    a. to some degree are unshrunk
    b. are the best
    c. can do everything better than others
    d. are quite significant

4. He who is faithful in a very little thing is faithful also:
    a. in all things
    b. to his church
    c. to man
    d. in much

QUOTE:

"The Lord said, 'He who is faithful in a very little thing is faithful also in much' (Luke 16:10). We must simply do the thing God tells us and not envy others and their tasks. We seek to do some great thing for God; but God wants us to do little things as though they were great."

5. We must fill the size of the need before us without envying:
   a. the greener grass
   b. a larger hole
   c. our pastor
   d. the tasks of others

6. God has one goal with us:
   a. to shrink us
   b. to create us in the image of Christ
   c. to clothe and feed us
   d. to teach us to worship

SESSION FIVE:

BECOMING A DWELLING

PLACE FOR GOD

Thus says the Lord,

"Heaven is My throne, and the earth is My footstool. Where then is a house you could build for Me? And where is a place that I may rest? For My hand made all these things, Thus all these things came into being," declares the Lord. But to this one I will look, To him who is humble and contrite of spirit, and who trembles at My word. —Isaiah 66:1–3

SESSION FIVE AUDIO MESSAGES:

5a. Becoming More Humble Than I Planned (part 1)
5b. Becoming More Humble Than I Planned (part 2)

ANSWER KEY TO LAST SESSION'S
SELF TEST QUESTIONS:

CHAPTER SEVEN. Brokenness Creates Openness
1.b, 2.c, 3.c, 4.c, 5.d, 6.a, 7.c., 8.d.
CHAPTER EIGHT. The Unshrunk Cloth
1.c, 2.b, 3.a, 4.d, 5.d, 6.b.

CHAPTER NINE

A PLACE
FOR HIM TO REST

In the kingdom, there are no great men of God, just humble men whom God has chosen to use greatly. How do we know when we are humble? When God speaks, we tremble. God is looking for a man who trembles at His Word. Such a man will find the Spirit of God resting upon him; he will become a dwelling place for the Almighty.

ENTERING THE SABBATH REST OF GOD

Heaven is My throne, and the earth is My footstool. Where then is a house you could build for Me? And where is a place that I may rest?   —Isaiah 66:1

God asks for nothing but ourselves. Our beautiful church buildings, our slick professionalism, all are nearly useless to God. He does not want what we have; He wants who we are. He seeks to create in our hearts a sanctuary for Himself, a place where He may rest.

In the Scriptures this *rest* is called "the Sabbath rest." It does not, however, come from keeping the Sabbath, for the Jews kept the Sabbath, but they never entered God's rest. The book of Hebrews is plain: Joshua did not give the Israelites rest (see Heb 4:7–8). After so long a period of Sabbath-keeping, the Scripture continues, "There remains therefore a Sabbath rest for the people of God" (Heb 4:9). This rest was something beyond keeping the seventh day holy.

The question must be asked then, "What is this Sabbath rest?" Let us explore Genesis in pursuit of our answer. "Then God blessed the seventh day and sanctified it, because in it He rested from all His work" (Gen 2:3). Before God rested on the Sabbath, there was nothing special or holy about the seventh day. Had the Lord rested on the third day, then it would have been holy. *Rest is not in the Sabbath, it is in God.* Rest is a prevailing quality of His completeness.

Revelation 4:6 describes the throne of God as having before it, as it were, "a sea of glass, like crystal." A sea of glass is a sea without waves or ripples, a symbol of the imperturbable calm of God. Let us grasp this point: *the Sabbath was not a source of rest for God; He was the Source of rest for the Sabbath.* As it is written, "the Creator of the ends of the earth does not become weary or tired" (Isa 40:28). And even as the Sabbath became holy when God rested upon it, so we become holy as we put away sin, as the fullness of God settles and rests upon us.

In our study, we are not associating God's rest merely with the sense of being rebuilt or rejuvenated, which we obviously need and associate with human rest. The rest we seek is not a rejuvenation of our energy, it is the *exchange* of energy: our life for God's, through which the vessel of our humanity is filled with the Divine Presence and all-sufficiency of Christ Himself.

ENVELOPED AND PERMEATED WITH GOD

The Hebrew word for *rest* was "nuach." One of several definitions meant "to rest, remain, be quiet." It also indicated a "complete envelopment and thus permeation," as in the spirit of Elijah "resting" on Elisha, or when wisdom "rests in the heart of him who has understanding." God is not looking for a place where He can merely cease from His labors with men. He seeks a relationship where He can "completely envelop and thus permeate" every dimension of our lives; where He can tabernacle, remain, and be quiet within us.

When God's rest abides upon us, we live in union with Jesus the same way He lived in union with the Father (see John 10:14–15). Christ's thought-life was "completely enveloped and thus permeated" with the Presence of God. He did only those things He saw and heard His Father do. He declared, "the Father abiding in Me does His works" (John 14:10). There is *rest* because it is *Christ working through us!* Jesus promises us, "If you ask Me anything in My name, I will do it" (John 14:14). How vain we are to think we can do miracles, love our enemies, or do any of the works of God without Christ doing His works through us!

This is why Jesus said, "Come to Me . . . and I will give you rest" (Matt 11:28). In a storm-tossed boat on the sea of Galilee, Christ's terrified disciples came to Him. Their cries were the cries of men about to die. Jesus rebuked the tempest, and immediately the wind and sea became "perfectly calm"—even as calm as He was (Matt 8:26). What program, what degree of ministerial professionalism can compare with the life and power we receive through Him?

You see, our efforts, no matter how much we spend of ourselves, cannot produce the rest or life of God. *We must come to Him.* Many leaders have worked themselves nearly to exhaustion seeking to serve God. If they spent half their time *with Him,* in prayer and waiting before Him, they would find His supernatural accompaniment working mightily in their efforts. They would become passengers in the vehicle of His will, a vehicle in which He Himself is both Captain and Navigator.

CEASE STRIVING, KNOW, THEN OBEY

To enter God's rest requires we abide in full surrender to His will, in perfect trust of His power. We learn to rest from our works "as God did from His" (Heb 4:10). It requires diligence, however, to enter God's rest (see Heb 4:11). To "rest from our labors" does not mean we have stopped working; it means we have stopped the laborious work of the flesh and sin. It means we have entered the eternal works which He brings forth through us.

The turmoil caused by unbelief is brought to rest by faith. The strife rooted in unforgiveness is removed by love. Our fearful thoughts, He arrests through trust; our many questions are answered by His wisdom. Such is the mind which has entered the rest of God.

The church needs to possess the knowledge of God's ways, for herein do we enter His rest (see Heb 3:8–12). We gain such knowledge through obedience to God's Word during conflicts. As we obey God through the testings of life, we learn how to deal with situations as God would. Consequently, it is of the utmost value to hear what God is speaking to us, and especially so when life seems to be a wilderness of hardship and trials.

Therefore, the Spirit says,

Today if you hear His voice, do not harden your hearts as when they provoked Me, as in the day of trial in the wilderness. . . . Therefore I was angry with this generation, and said, "They always go astray in their heart; and they did not know My ways"; as I swore in My wrath, they shall not enter My rest.   —Hebrews 3:7–8, 10–11

He says, "They always go astray in their heart . . . they did not know My ways . . . they shall not enter My rest." Let us understand: *Knowing God's ways leads to His rest.*

We must see that there is no rest in a hardened heart. There is no rest when we rebel against God. Our rest comes from becoming honest about our needs and allowing Christ to change us.

Thus Jesus said, "Learn from Me . . . and you shall find rest for your souls" (Matt 11:29). Stop fighting with God and learn from Him! Let His Word put to death the torments of the sin nature. Cease struggling, cease wrestling against the Blessed One. Trust Him! For eventually His Word will plunder the defenses of your heart. Be committed to your surrender! In time He shall no longer use adversity to reach your heart, for you shall delight in being vulnerable to Him. Continue your diligent yielding until even His whisper brings sweet trembling to your soul. Far more precious than the men of a hundred nations is one man perfectly given to the Spirit of God. This man is God's tabernacle, the one to whom God looks . . . and is well-pleased.

He says, "Heaven is My throne, and the earth is My footstool. Where then is a house you could build for Me? And where is a place that I may rest? For My hand made all these things, thus all these things came into being" (Isa 66:1–2). Yet, incredibly, one man with one quality of heart captures the attention and promise of God. "But to this one I will look, to him who is humble and contrite of spirit, and who trembles at My word" (v 2).

God looks to the man who trembles when He speaks. For in him the holy power of the Most High can, without striving, abide in perfect peace. He has learned the ways of God; he delights in obedience. He has chosen to give God what He asks: nothing less than all he is. In return, this man becomes a place, a holy place, where God Himself can rest.

Be commited to your surrender! shall be delight in being vulnerable.

Let's pray: *Heavenly Father, how I desire to be permeated and enveloped by Your Presence. I confess I am anxious and untrusting. Forgive me, O God, for a withdrawing heart. Shape me to become a dwelling place for You!*

—FROM THE BOOK,
HOLINESS, TRUTH AND THE PRESENCE OF GOD

SELF TEST, CHAPTER NINE

Remember, we are looking for answers that correspond with this training. Please write out your essay answers, allowing the Holy Spirit to provoke your thoughts. You may want to use them for group discussion. Note: we do not provide answers to essay questions. To check your multiple choice answers, see answer key in the next session.

Chapter 9, Essay #1: Explain where the rest of the Sabbath is.

Chapter 9, Essay #2: What are two renderings of the Hebrew word "nuach?"

1. God does not want what we have; He wants who we are. God asks for nothing but:
   a. professionalism
   b. ourselves
   c. sacrifices
   d. good works

2. Rest is not in the Sabbath, it is:
   a. throughout the entire week
   b. when we sleep
   c. in God
   d. in us

3. Revelation 4:6 describes the throne of God as having before it, as it were:
   a. kings and queens
   b. a sea of glass, like crystal
   c. huge steps
   d. scepters of all colors

4. The rest we seek is not a rejuvenation of our energy, it is the _____ of our energy for God's.
   a. exchange
   b. substitution
   c. glorification
   d. impossibility

5. The Father abiding in _____ does His works (John 14:10).
   a. the church
   b. my neighbors
   c. plans and programs
   d. Me

6. As we _____ God through the testings of life, we learn how to deal with situations as God would.
   a. murmur to
   b. obey
   c. wrestle with
   d. question

7. Knowing God's ways leads to:
   a. no tribulations
   b. omnipotence
   c. Bethlehem
   d. His rest

8. God looks for a man who _____, and this man becomes a place where God Himself can rest.
   a. keeps busy with His work
   b. trembles at God's Word
   c. delights in obedience
   d. both b & c

QUOTE:

"How do we know when we are humble? When God speaks, we tremble. God is looking for a man who trembles at His Word. Such a man will find the Spirit of God resting upon him; he will become a dwelling place for the Almighty."

CHAPTER TEN

WHAT YOU GIVE OVER, GOD WILL TAKE OVER

Early this morning the Lord gave me a special word that I hope will be as living to you as it was to me. At the moment of my awakening, the Holy Spirit spoke to my heart, "What you give over, I will take over."

THE MARRIAGE OF FAITH AND HUMILITY

We cannot advance spiritually without both faith and humility. Indeed, faith without humility inevitably becomes presumption, while humility without faith never ascends above oppression.

Consider: Faith's nature, in part, is to possess the promises of God. Israel was commanded by the Almighty to possess the Promised Land. Scriptures tell us that without faith it is impossible to please God and that whatever is done without faith is sin (see Heb 11:6; Rom 14:23). Thus, faith unites the human heart to God. As a result, the sinful appropriate God's righteousness and those who were dead gain access to God's life. Christianity without faith is like a computer without electricity: the circuits of "proper knowledge" may be in place, but there is no light, no power nor functionality.

Yet, where faith possesses, humility surrenders. Consider Christ as our example. There will be a time when every knee will bow and tongue confess that Jesus Christ is Lord (see Phil 2:10–11); the kingdoms of this world will finally become the kingdom of our Lord (see Rev 11:15). However, Christ's reaction to subduing the world is that He then "delivers up the kingdom to the . . . Father" (1 Cor 15:24). This is the humility of Christ: what He conquers, He then surrenders. In America we want the first part, having faith to conquer, but we're not sure we want the second part, giving it back to God. Yet, this is the pattern of those who have followed God: Abraham believes God and a son is born; humility takes Isaac, and offers him back to God. David conquers Jerusalem, then dedicates it to the Lord, calling it the "city of God."

You see, the motive behind the exercise of our faith must mature until what we've appropriated through faith becomes an offering we now surrender back to God. Our goal is not only to create a better life here, but, through surrender, to extend the kingdom of God to earth. Faith brings to earth heaven's provisions; surrender brings God's Presence into those provisions.

OUR TITHE AND GOD'S HEART

So, what we give over to God He promises to take over. Here is where true faith expands into the higher levels of Christlikeness. Yet conversely, we should also realize: what we withhold from God, we also isolate from His ability to inhabit and multiply. This is why the Bible says our tithe is holy unto the Lord. If we give a minimum of one tenth of our income back to God and His purposes, we are releasing into His hands the opportunity for supernatural supply.

I'm not merely talking about money, but faith and surrender. However, tithing is a big part of our becoming complete in God. Why? We demonstrate that our trust is in God. You say, "Pastor Francis, are you trying to put your hand in my pocket?" No, I'm trying to put your hand in God's pocket, where you are able to prosper not in the accumulation of things, but in the expansion of God in all the things of your life.

I have nothing to gain from you in teaching this. I don't take a salary from our church and the housing allowance I receive, I then surrender to the work of the Lord. What my faith possesses, my humility surrenders. Likewise, I desire that you also enjoy the best that God has for you.

You say, "But I'm not making enough to tithe. I'm going to run out of money." Well, if you think you're going to run out anyway, run out into God's arms, run out trusting Him. In fact, He promises,

> "Bring the whole tithe into the storehouse, so that there may be food in My house, and test Me now in this," says the Lord of hosts, "if I will not open for you the windows of heaven, and pour out for you a blessing until it overflows.
>
> "Then I will rebuke the devourer for you, so that it may not destroy the fruits of the ground; nor will your vine in the field cast *its grapes,*" says the Lord of hosts. And all the nations will call you blessed.
> —Malachi 3:10–12

Again, I'm not talking about money alone, but the issues that speak of the very quality of our lives. Many are suffering from a spiritual "devourer," an enemy that drains away energy, time and resources so that you never seem to have enough. The Lord is saying, "Turn over your finances to Me and I will turn over My resources to you. I will destroy that which is destroying you."

There's a wonderful story that exemplifies this principle of faith and surrender. During a terrible famine, the Lord told Elijah to "Go to Zarephath . . . behold, I have commanded a widow there to provide for you" (1 Kings 17:9). Please note, the Lord did not command a wealthy businessman to provide for Elijah, but a destitute widow. We enter the story with the woman, facing starvation, about to prepare a meager last meal for herself and her son. Yet, though she is not an Israelite, she greets Elijah with faith, saying, "As the Lord your God lives. . ." (v 12)

God's way to activate her faith and to bring her into a supernatural provision was to require her to give over the little she had to fulfill the purpose of God. What seemed like an insensitive, even cruel command: Elijah ordered her to feed him first, and then take food for herself. Although she knew not the plan and provision of God, Elijah knew and he urged her into both faith and surrender. As a result, God provided for her miraculously: "The bowl of flour was not exhausted nor did the jar of oil become empty" until the famine broke (v 16).

GIVE WHEN YOU ARE POOR

Denise and I had a time in our lives when we were nearly destitute. Yet, even when we had little, we always tithed. We honored the Lord from the first of our increase. Our giving in faith and surrender gave us many testimonies of the Lord. Remember, when Jesus fed the 5,000, the original five loaves and two fish came from a little boy. He could have hoarded his little stock of food, but he didn't. Instead, he turned them over to the Lord and God took over in power.

When I hear people say, "I can't afford to give," I immediately say, "Listen, you can't afford not to give." When faith is activated and surrender per-fected, God steps into our lives. I want you to have a testimony of God's supply, where each of us can say, "God came through for me." I'm not saying that we must abandon common sense, but remem-ber, Jesus multiplied the little in a time of need. God multiplied the widow's provisions during a drought. Maybe it's in the times of need that we should surrender the most.

The faith God develops as we give is the same faith that comes through us when we lay hands on the sick. Our faithfulness with money shows Jesus that we can be trusted with greater things such as miracles. Why live in the pitiful little realm of un-belief when we can have the provisions of the Most High?

Recently, I spoke at a conference in Mississippi. Our host, a pastor from Jackson, was only going to be able to attend one meeting due to a business commitment that was going to take him to South America for a week. The trip would have prob-ably secured a financial increase, yet the Lord spoke to this young man to stay at the conference. Strug-gling at first, he decided to obey the Lord and put his income into God's hands. One hour after he decided to stay, he received a phone call from Rus-sia for an order that was the largest his company ever had, which would keep them busy for the fol-lowing year!

CHRIST OUR PATTERN

The key to how Jesus always had what He needed is revealed in John 17:10. Praying to the Father, Jesus said, "All things that are Mine are Thine." Jesus surrendered all. Thus, He could con-tinue with confidence in His prayer, "and [what things are] Thine are Mine." So, also with us: Make this a sincere act of surrender.

Beloved, whatever we have was God's in the first place anyway. To those who give all to Him,

He says, "What's Mine is thine." We exchange our little for God's much. Whether it is with our finances, our families, our future or our past, the key to unlocking the destiny of God is faith and surrender. What we give over, He will take over.

Let's pray: *Lord Jesus, continue to teach me to surrender. I want to be a giver, like You. What an awesome, divine exchange, as my life becomes Yours.*

—FROM THE *ICIT* WEEKLY MAILER

SELF TEST, CHAPTER TEN
Remember, we are looking for answers that correspond with this training. Please write out your essay answers, allowing the Holy Spirit to provoke your thoughts. You may want to use them for group discussion. Note: we do not provide answers to essay questions. To check your multiple choice answers, see answer key in the next session.

Chapter 10, Essay #1: What does the Scripture mean that says God will rebuke the devourer (see Mal 3:10–12)?

Chapter 10, Essay #2: Why is it important to give when we are poor?

1. To advance spiritually we must have:
    a. presumption
    b. faith
    c. humility
    d. both b & c

2. Christ's example, and the pattern of those who have followed God, is having faith to _____ and humility to _____.
    a. become mature, stay as we are
    b. speak, be silent
    c. appropriate, surrender
    d. build a ministry, get others to help with leadership of it

3. What we withhold from God, we also isolate from His ability to:
    a. inhabit and multiply
    b. take away
    c. control
    d. cover up

4. When we surrender our tithe back to God, we are acting in faith and trust, and allowing Him to:
    a. lead us to the right church
    b. bless our pastor
    c. see our good deed
    d. supernaturally supply our needs

5. The statement, "What we give over to God He promises to take over," is not talking about money alone, but about:
    a. the issues that speak of the very quality of our lives
    b. what stock or banks we invest our money in
    c. what insurance we have
    d. all the above

6. Pastor Francis refers to a "spiritual devourer" as being:
    a. a communist leader with hunger and famine in their land
    b. an enemy that drains away our energy, time and resources so that we never seem to have enough
    c. a person really hungry for the Word
    d. a tape player that eats our spiritual teaching tapes

7. How did God activate the Zarephath widow's faith (1 Kings 17:9) and bring her into supernatural provision?
    a. by causing her to be afraid
    b. He sent a wealthy Israelite to encourage her
    c. by having Elijah provide for her
    d. He required her to give over the little she had for His purpose

8. What is Christ's pattern for us in John 17:10?
    a. a sincere act of surrendering all
    b. knowing that all He possessed was God's, and God's possessions were His
    c. keeping quiet about our need
    d. both a & b

QUOTE:

"What we give over to God He promises to take over. Here is where true faith expands into the higher levels of Christlikeness."

Session Six:

Humility:

Flexible in Service

to the Holy Spirit

The wind blows where it wishes and you hear the sound of it, but do not know where it comes from and where it is going; so is everyone who is born of the Spirit.   —John 3:8

SESSION SIX AUDIO MESSAGES:

6a. Perfectly Weak
6b. The Spirit of Grace

ANSWER KEY TO LAST SESSION'S
SELF TEST QUESTIONS:

CHAPTER NINE. A Place For Him to Rest
1.b, 2.c, 3.b, 4.a, 5.d, 6.b, 7.d, 8.d.
CHAPTER TEN. What You Give Over,
God Will Take Over
1.d, 2.c, 3.a, 4.d, 5.a, 6.b, 7.d, 8.d.

CHAPTER ELEVEN

SURRENDER OF THE VISION-KEEPER

To walk with God is to walk a path of increasing surrender and trust. Indeed, the time is at hand when the Lord Jesus shall confront our tendencies to control Him. Not only will we know doctrinally that Christ is Lord, but we will also serve Him as Lord.

CHURCHES IN TRANSITION

If you find yourself more drawn toward prayer than promotion, more toward humility than hype, you are being prepared by the Lord for the glory of God. What He is working in you is typical of what God is establishing in thousands of other believers.

However, before the Father ultimately reveals Christ as Lord over the earth, He will first reveal Him as Lord over the church. And while we should rejoice, we must also take heed. For until we are standing face-to-face in glory with Jesus Himself, we are going to be in transition. To each of us, Christ's call remains, "Come, follow Me!" (Luke 18:22) If we will walk with Him in obedience, He will take us into the fullness of His Presence.

once satw experience it, you want it fou itou.

Blessings a Tomauar

Still, transitions can be frightening. The uncertainty of those passages between spiritual plateaus can hold us hostage to yesterday's blessings. Let us recall with godly fear that the bronze serpent, which brought healing to Israel in the wilderness, by Hezekiah's day had become an idol which had to be torn down. Our hearts must bow to God alone, for even spiritual gifts when isolated from Christ, the Giver, can become idolatrous.

Therefore, to successfully navigate this season of change, the Lord will require of us a fresh surrender to His Lordship. He will demand that our preconceived ideas and expectations be submitted to Him. For if we are continually telling the Holy Spirit where we expect to go, we neutralize our capacity to hear where He wants to take us.

CHRIST IN US

To better understand the changes God is initiating in the church, we are going to study the life of Mary, Jesus' mother. More than any other woman, God had blessed Mary. She alone was granted the wondrous privilege of giving birth to the Son of God.

While the Lord's promise and purpose with Mary were unparalleled, in two significant ways His promise to us is similar. First, even as Mary received Christ into her physical body, we have received Jesus into our spirits. And secondly, as she birthed Christ, our quest is to see Jesus unfettered from the womb of our religion about Him. Our destiny is not just to carry Christ inside but to reveal the fullness of His glory in this world.

Even now, abiding within our spirits, deeper and more profound than our church doctrines, is the actual Spirit of Christ. The consequence of this union of Christ's Spirit with our spirits expands the original seven creation days into the eighth day. We are new creatures in a new creation (see Gal

6:15). In this new beginning to God's eternal plan, Jesus Christ is the firstborn of a new race of men (see 1 Cor 15:45).

As Jesus was both God and man, so the church is actually the dwelling of Christ in the temple of man. There is not a different Jesus in us than He who dwells in heaven. He is Christ wrapped in glory in heaven; He is Christ wrapped in our human flesh on earth.

Our salvation is nothing less than the Perfect One dwelling in imperfect ones, the Almighty abiding in the feeble, the All-Sufficient God dwelling among insufficient people. This is the mystery and glory of our salvation: *Christ in His completeness extends Himself into our lives!*

Crucial to the success of His mission is our receiving these truths with faith, determining that they shall be our *reality*, not just our *theology*. It is here, in this carrying of the actual Presence of Christ within us, that we share with Mary the awe of God's purpose for us.

JESUS IN SUBJECTION

While Joseph was a good man, it was Mary who nurtured Jesus and continued to raise Him after Joseph died. In fact, we shall see that Mary became the matriarch of the family. Uniquely, under her spiritual influence, Jesus matured. It was natural that, over time, Mary would consider herself the "Keeper of the Vision; Guardian of Him Who is to Come," for, in truth, she was.

"And He continued in subjection to them" (Luke 2:51). This is an astonishing thought: Jesus, Lord of heaven, in subjection to a lowly carpenter and his wife. Yet if we think about it, is it not equally astonishing that the rule of Christ in His church is, at least in part, subject to our initiatives? He submits Himself to our schedules and to our service times. He works within the confinements of our weaknesses and temperaments. Yet, we should honestly ask ourselves, is it a voice from heaven or the traditions of earth which determines how long we shall worship Him on Sunday morning?

If the Lord so decided, in an instant He could reveal His majesty and draw trembling surrender from all mankind. However, He restrains Himself, choosing not to intimidate but to inspire our obedience. He has chosen to hide His glory not *from* us but *in* us. And then, in order to perfect our character, He subjects Himself to our initiatives of hunger and faith.

However, the fact that Jesus will *accommodate* and submit Himself to the conditions we offer Him does not mean that He has approved of our limitations upon Him. The standard of the church is not the church; it is Christ. And this is our present dilemma: Just as Jesus subjected Himself to Mary and Joseph and they became, for a time, the "Vision-Keepers," so we have assumed that Christ will continue to exist in "subjection" to us. He will not. For as Jesus arises in His Lordship, to save us He must first deliver us from our efforts to control Him.

A TIME TO LET GO

It is significant that Mary still exercised matriarchal supervision over Jesus even after He was a mature man. At the wedding feast in Cana we find Jesus, His disciples, and Mary, the "Vision-Keeper." "They have no wine," Mary told her son. Jesus answered, "Woman, what do I have to do with you? My hour has not yet come" (John 2:3–4). In spite of what Jesus just said, Mary tells the servants, "Whatever He says to you, do it" (v 5). While I am amazed at the fact that the Father worked through Mary's orchestration of this miracle, the fact is, Jesus did not come forth to do the will of

His mother but His Father. It was time for Jesus, Mary's son, to begin His ministry as Jesus, God's Son.

A significant and necessary reversal of authority was needed in Mary's relationship with Christ—a change which she had not anticipated. In her mind, her sense of influence was simply a continuation of her God-given responsibility as Vision-Keeper.

The problem of control worsened after the miracle at Cana: "After this He went down to Capernaum, He and His mother, and His brothers, and His disciples; and there they stayed a few days" (John 2:12). The verse reads, "He and His mother" went to Capernaum. Do you see? Mary, the "Keeper of the Vision," has taken what she thinks is a legitimate position, an earned place of influence, with Christ.

In defense of Mary, she clearly has been with Jesus the longest; she has paid the highest price. More than anyone, she has heard the Word and believed it; her faith has borne Christ Himself! She has magnificently served the purposes of God. Perhaps she had every right to think that Christ could work the miracles as long as she remained a guiding influence. Her continued "mothering" was not evil but natural.

However, God had determined it was time for Jesus to be unfettered from all human influences of control. Jesus would now only do the things He saw His Father do.

This, I believe, is where God is jealously directing us: We are being emptied of our agendas, false expectations, and nonbiblical traditions so that Christ alone will be Lord over the church. What we are learning is that, even though we have served as keepers of the vision, before our hopes can be fulfilled we must surrender afresh to the Lord of the vision.

A SWORD WILL PIERCE YOUR HEART

It should be noted that the plans of God are full of surprises. No matter how true a vision from God may be, it will never be fulfilled in the manner in which we have imagined. All our expectations are incomplete. In fact, our very ideas often become the most subtle obstacles standing between us and our appointed future in God. Thus, we must keep our minds open and submitted to God, for when God fulfills His Word, it is always "exceeding abundantly beyond all that we ask or think" (Eph 3:20).

We've been talking of Mary and her role as "Keeper of the Vision." Now we will discuss how the Lord shifts our identity from control to complete surrender.

Interestingly, the first stage in Christ's preparation of Mary finds Him resisting her. Before the Lord can bring any of us into a new phase of our destiny, He must dismantle the "sense of attainment" which often accompanies our previous relationship to His will. It is a fact that many church movements, both in and out of denominations, began simply. Hungry souls longed for, and found, more of God. Over time, as their numbers grew, success replaced hunger; people grew more satisfied with God's blessings than with His Presence. There is a profound difference.

The apostle Paul illuminates this phenomenon, using Israel as an example. He writes, "Israel . . . failed to reach their goal. And why? Because their minds were fixed on what they achieved instead of on what they believed" (Rom 9:31–32 PHILLIPS).

What happened to Israel is typical of us all. Without realizing it, we find ourselves relying upon what we have achieved. The Bible says that God resists the proud but He gives grace to the humble (see James 4:6). It is always His mercy which guides our gaze away from our attainments and back to the knowledge of our need.

Today, people from many streams of Christian thought are beginning to acknowledge their own personal shortcomings. The fact is, *we all need correction!* And the beginning of that process is found in Jesus resisting our pride and restoring to us a fresh hunger to know Him.

Thus, in order to ultimately lift Mary higher, Jesus must lower her opinion of herself: He resists her on her present level. It is interesting that, in response to His resistance, Mary's need to control seems to grow more aggressive.

> And He came home, and the multitude gathered again, to such an extent that they could not even eat a meal. And when His own people heard of this, they went out to take custody of Him; for they were saying, "He has lost His senses."
>
> —Mark 3:20–21

These are strong words: "take custody . . . He has lost His senses." It is likely that the prevailing influence over Christ's relatives has come from Mary. Has her unrest caused their unrest? The issue is not that Jesus has lost His senses but that they have lost control. For Jesus to take control, we must lose control. Revival is as simple as that.

We should be aware that, when the real Christ begins to unveil Himself to His church, He will first reduce us from being achievers to becoming followers again. The very power of Christ to heal, deliver, and work miracles is contained in the revelation of His Lordship. *Deny Him His sovereignty in your church and you deny your church His power.* He cannot be manipulated, bribed, or begged. Remember, Jesus did no miracle until He began to manifest Himself as Lord. From that time on, the only relationships He actively sustained were those which recognized and submitted to His Lordship over them.

The very next scene in Mark's gospel begins, "And His mother and His brothers arrived" (Mark

3:31). We can imagine that, outwardly, Mary is subtly but clearly in charge. Inwardly, she is probably troubled and insecure. Jesus, surrounded by a multitude, is told, "Behold, Your mother and Your brothers are outside looking for You" (Mark 3:32). The implied undertone is, *There is someone here with something more important than what you are now doing.*

In any other scheme of things, it might be right to honor one's family with special privileges, but not above doing the will of God. Mary is outside looking in. For what may be the first time in her life, she feels a spiritual distance between herself and her Son. We should see that the more we set ourselves to control another person, the less intimate we can be with them; for intimacy is found in vulnerability and surrender, not in control. Of all those near to Jesus, Mary and family have slipped the farthest away; they are *outside* the sphere of intimate fellowship.

When Jesus was told His mother had arrived, He took the opportunity to end this stage of their relationship by saying,

> "Who are My mother and My brothers?" And looking about on those who were sitting around Him, He said, "Behold, My mother and My brothers! For whoever does the will of God, he is My brother and sister and mother."   —Mark 3:33–35

Though they were outside, they were close enough to hear His rebuke. Right there, the word spoken to Mary thirty years earlier by Simeon was fulfilled: A sword pierced her heart and her inner thoughts were revealed (see Luke 2:35). Christ surgically and mercifully removed from Mary the stronghold of control.

Today, God is surgically removing from us that which seeks to control Christ. It was for Mary's good that Jesus cut her off. It was for her gain that He destroyed that which unconsciously opposed Him. There are times in our walk with God that it is good for the Lord to cut off old attitudes which have limited His freedom to change us. If we are truly His disciples, we will not merely survive His rebuke; we will bear more fruit under His pruning.

As the day of His return nears, expect to see many changes. Our destiny is to become the body of Christ with Jesus as the head. The church was created to receive its directives from a living relationship with Him. There is no other way for us to be led by Him than through seeking Him in prayer and receiving His Word in contriteness of heart.

CHRIST AS LORD OVER ALL

Jesus is not being cruel when He terminates our efforts to control Him. Did He not command us, "Whoever serves me must follow me"? Yet, with His command, was there not this promise: "Where I am, my servant also will be" (John 12:26 NIV). If we follow Him, we will abide in fellowship with Him. His refusal to be controlled by our efforts is an answer to our deepest desires. We have prayed and labored to see the real Jesus emerge through the church—and He is! But He is coming as *Lord*.

At the same time, a caution is in order. This transition is not a green light to usurp the authority of the pastor; this is not an excuse to justify lawlessness in the church. If we will all posture ourselves in prayer, ministering to Jesus as Lord, as did the leaders in Acts 13:1–3, we are going to see the most magnificent demonstrations of God's power and glory.

If we want our Christianity to truly have Christ, we must let Him rule. Certainly, there will be a thrusting of our lives into greater dependency. Yes, we will be forced to embrace the most drastic of changes. Without doubt, we will be reduced to what seems like the beginnings of our walk with

God. Yet, we shall also regain the passions of our soul in earnest seeking of the Almighty! And oh! How such seeking pleases Him!

Biblically, this state of heart is called "first love," and there is no reality of God in our lives without it. You see, His arms are not short that He cannot reach to our churches and cities. The privilege the Lord is granting us is to enter the most profoundly wonderful, most unpredictably glorious experience we can have: *to know the power of the living God!* In such knowledge all reality is filled with meaning. What once seemed vague is now clearly unveiled as a fulfillment of the Word of God!

But the power of God is also frightening. There is something about the actual Presence of God when He supernaturally interacts with mankind that has no parallel in mere religion. It is a time of power but also of great carefulness. Not only do the dead come alive, but also the living may, as did Ananias and Sapphira, fall dead. It is the most exultant, yet fearful, thing! Like the women at Christ's tomb, it is a world filled with "fear and great joy" (Matt 28:8). Such is our Christian experience when Jesus is Lord over His church!

What is perhaps most wonderful about serving the Lord is that, even when we fail and fall short, He remains true to His purpose in our lives. With Him, correction is not rejection. Although His hands wound, they also heal.

The end of our story about Mary is this: On the day of Pentecost, Mary and Jesus' brothers were all part of the 120 in the upper room. Scripture mentions Mary by name (see Acts 1:14).

Mary truly proved herself to be a bondslave of the Lord. Here was this remarkable woman, humbled and broken but once again serving God on the highest level of yieldedness. What she wanted from the beginning, she obtained: *deep intimacy with Christ.* Yet, she reached her goal not by striving or trying to control Jesus but by surrendering to Him.

In the richest way, through the Holy Spirit, Mary again had Jesus living inside her. She learned the secret of being a humble follower, not a controller of the Lord Jesus Christ in the day of His glory.

Let's pray: *Lord Jesus, it is an indescribable honor to follow You. May I know, by Your Spirit, when to hang on and when to let go—when to birth a vision and when to surrender it back to You.*

—FROM THE BOOK, *The Days of His Presence*

SELF TEST, CHAPTER ELEVEN
Remember, we are looking for answers that correspond with this training. Please write out your essay answers, allowing the Holy Spirit to provoke your thoughts. You may want to use them for group discussion. Note: we do not provide answers to essay questions. To check your multiple choice answers, see answer key in the next session.

Chapter 11, Essay #1: Why must the Lord dismantle the "sense of attainment"?

Chapter 11, Essay #2: The text states that Jesus is not being cruel when He terminates our efforts to control Him. What does this mean?

1. What happens if we are not submitting our preconceived ideas and expectations to the Lord and if we are telling the Holy Spirit where we expect to go?
   a. We move ahead faster in our ministry and goals
   b. We neutralize our capacity to hear where He wants to take us
   c. We can navigate more smoothly through a season of change
   d. We get a fresh surrender reward

2. In what way is the Lord's promise to us similar to His promise and purpose with Mary, Jesus' mother?
   a. our quest is to unfetter Jesus from our religion about Him
   b. to carry Christ inside and to reveal the fullness of His glory in this world
   c. we have received Jesus into our spirits
   d. all the above

3. Just as with Mary and Joseph, Jesus subjects Himself (at least in part) to our initiatives and schedules, for a time. Which of the following statements pertaining to this is true?
   a. As Christ arises in Lordship, He must deliver us from our efforts to control Him
   b. Christ will always continue to exist in "subjection" to us
   c. We are like Vision-Keepers, for a time
   d. both a & c

4. Like Mary, we can anticipate a significant and necessary reversal of _____ in our relationship with Christ, letting Him come forth.
   a. time
   b. authority
   c. giving
   d. diet

5. No matter how true a vision from God may be:
   a. our expectations are incomplete
   b. it will never be fulfilled in the manner in which we have imagined
   c. we must never give in to correction
   d. both a & b

6. The fulfillment of the word spoken to Mary, *"A sword will pierce even your own soul—to the end that thoughts from many hearts may be revealed"* (Luke 2:35), was when Christ:
   a. told everyone what she was thinking
   b. handed her a sword to do warfare
   c. removed from her the stronghold of control
   d. had compassion and let her continue being His guiding influence

7. If we want our Christianity to truly have Christ:
   a. we will be reduced to what seems like the beginnings of our walk with God
   b. we must let Him rule
   c. we will be forced to embrace drastic changes
   d. all the above

8. We reach our goal of deep intimacy with Christ by:
   a. staying in full-time ministry
   b. being a humble follower and not a controller
   c. surrendering to Him
   d. both b & c

QUOTE:

"If the Lord so decided, in an instant He could reveal His majesty and draw trembling surrender from all mankind. However, He restrains Himself, choosing not to intimidate but to inspire our obedience."

CHAPTER TWELVE

TO DELIGHT
IN HIDDENNESS

The desire to be acknowledged and appreciated by others is basic to human nature. Jesus Himself seemed somewhat troubled that, after healing ten lepers, only one returned to give thanks (see Luke 17). Yet, while the need to be occasionally appreciated is not sin, it can become sin when we begin seeking recognition. We must determine that our service to mankind is guided by a higher, more focused obedience to God.

Jesus lived solely for the glory of God. We, however, too often seek the glory and praise of man. In spite of the fact that Jesus repeatedly affirmed that the Father, who sees in secret, will reward us openly (see Matt 6), we remain offended if we do not receive credit for our good deeds. This quest for recognition can become a source of wrong motives and failed endeavors; it can give a place to jealousy, pride and selfish ambition if we are not careful.

I wish I could say I have never walked in this type of human weakness, but that would be untrue. In fact, I experienced something a few years ago that, though quite painful at the time, ultimately unfolded into a wonderful revelation concerning the nature of the Holy Spirit. Yet, before I proceed, let me state that to share this publicly requires I make my own frailties visible before you. So, please grant me your grace.

The scene was the 1996 Promise Keeper's Atlanta convocation for pastors. This event was the largest gathering of pastors in North American history—more than 40,000 ministers united from a great variety of backgrounds and cultures. It featured two themes in which I had been quite active: unity and reconciliation. Although I had been instrumental in bringing thousands of pastors and leaders together in hundreds of cities, I had not been asked to participate in this conference. Although I mentioned my dilemma to no one, the lack of recognition was producing an ever deepening disturbance in my thought life.

I decided that, even though I had not been asked to serve, I would go to the conference. However, I relegated my struggle to a secret chamber in my soul, a place where wounds are stored while I continue on in God. I thought that perhaps, once I reached the conference, the Lord would open a door and call me to contribute more visibly.

But no door opened. Pastors who were familiar with my work would ask, "So, why aren't you speaking at this conference?" I'd smile and respond, "This must increase and I must decrease."

While my answer was both humble and sincere, I was becoming much more humble than I planned. The fact was, I was asking myself the same question: Why wasn't I speaking? Ghosts of past rejections began to manipulate my fears. So, while I attended the ministers' conference and truly rejoiced in the unity, I felt detached from it. I watched a spiritual dream that I carried in my soul emerge and take form, only to find myself floating, dreamlike, outside of the fulfillment. I was simultaneously deeply blessed and thoroughly miserable.

Finally, I laid my soul bare to a couple of friends. "What should I do?" I asked. "If I promote myself, God stands against me; if I remain silent, I sacrifice my contribution to this historic event." If nothing else, I knew the Lord was crucifying my pride and fleshly ambition. Indeed, beyond a legitimate desire to stir pastors and leaders toward greater unity, I must admit that there was another part of me that desired personal recognition.

The conference came and went, but my inner struggle stayed with me. After several months I successfully buried the conflict beneath my everyday thoughts. I was going on with my life. However, in May, the issue resurfaced, this time to be wonderfully resolved. I was at a Mission America meeting in Washington, D.C., listening as a friend shared over lunch how the Lord used other leaders to lay foundations in his life. As we talked, I began to see that I was not outside of what God was doing, but underneath it. My labors in Christ (and those of many others) were part of a divine substructure upon which this current work was unfolding.

The efforts of those who serve in high visibility today will likely become foundations for greater works by others tomorrow. I felt I was beginning to understand my role in the context of God's unfolding kingdom. I was even able to look at my own life and see individuals whose teachings and spiritual examples had become foundations in me—people whom I also had never thanked or acknowledged.

My need for recognition had diminished greatly, yet the Holy Spirit had something vital to add to me. That evening, as I sought God, I confessed my sin of seeking recognition. Immediately the Holy Spirit spoke to my heart a simple question concerning Himself. He asked, "Do you know My name?"

This was a God-moment, where one small introductory thought floods the soul with a river of revelation. I knew the primary revelation of the Father's name was Yahweh and the name of the Son, of course, is Jesus. I recalled all the "compound names" of God in the Bible, but again could not identify the actual name of the Holy Spirit. It struck me as profound that, in a lifetime of ministry, I could not remember once reading or hearing a teaching about the name of the Holy Spirit. I saw that every good work, every miracle of grace, every spiritual advancement I obtained, even those that came in spite of myself, had occurred through the work of the Holy Spirit. Yet, He never drew attention to Himself, choosing instead to direct my praise toward the Father or the Son. Amazingly, for all His work, I did not know His name or think to ask Him!

Then the revelation gloriously expanded. Suddenly, I realized that everything that was accomplished worldwide was the result of the Holy Spirit. Not one genuine virtue emerged in anyone apart from His working, whether it was concerning the prayer movement, reconciliation between denominations and races, the renewal, various revivals that had sprung forth throughout the world, or the increasing harvest of the nations—all was the work of the Holy Spirit. Yet, no one knew His name!

Still He was not done with me. I was even more astonished when I quickly searched my memory of the Scriptures and, to my knowledge, could recall no prophet, priest or king whom the Holy Spirit inspired to reveal His name! Did I know His name? No! Throughout history, from brooding over the pre-creation universe to strengthening the Son of God at the cross, He had accomplished all the work of the Godhead, yet He never revealed His name.

This truth hit me as a burning revelation. The nature of the Holy Spirit is in stark contrast to our human desires to be seen, praised and recognized. I saw how the Holy Spirit truly, passionately delights in hiddenness.

Then I saw the most wonderful unveiling of all: the passions of the Holy Spirit's heart. Two blazing fires consume His every thought: to see Jesus glorified and the Father's will accomplished on earth. Here, before my eyes, I saw perfect humility and complete obedience—the God-pattern that would lead me to spiritual rest and maturity.

Beloved, if we would truly be filled with the Spirit, we too must abandon the quest for recognition. God sees and knows our works. Whether or not a promotion comes in this world, the reward we must seek is that which comes from heaven. Until then, let us seek the fullness of the Holy Spirit, whose glorious delight is to work in hiddenness.

Let's pray: *Lord, forgive me for seeking recognition from man. Help me, blessed Holy Spirit, to be filled with Your substance—Your thoughts and motives, Your contentment and power. Live Your marvelous life of hiddenness through me, that Jesus may truly be glorified and the Father's will be fully accomplished.*

—FROM THE *ICIT* WEEKLY MAILER

SELF TEST, CHAPTER TWELVE

Remember, we are looking for answers that correspond with this training. Please write out your essay answers, allowing the Holy Spirit to provoke your thoughts. You may want to use them for group discussion. Note: we do not provide answers to essay questions. To check your multiple choice answers, see answer key at end of this session.

Chapter 12, Essay #1: What is so significant about no one knowing the Holy Spirit's name?

1. Our basic human nature and need to be appreciated can become a quest for recognition, which can be:
    a. a source of wrong motives and failed endeavors
    b. a healthy ambition
    c. the only way we get our needs met
    d. what keeps us focused in our ministry

QUOTE:

"I saw the most wonderful unveiling of all: the passions of the Holy Spirit's heart. Two blazing fires consume His every thought: to see Jesus glorified and the Father's will accomplished on earth. Here, before my eyes, I saw perfect humility and complete obedi-ence—the God-pattern that would lead me to spiritual rest and maturity."

2. We must determine that our service to mankind is guided by:
   a. the opinion of our friends
   b. obedience to God
   c. whether or not we have time
   d. whether our leaders will praise us

3. Our efforts in serving the Lord today can become _____ by others tomorrow.
   a. foundations for greater works
   b. obstacles
   c. ridiculous ideas
   d. a role that made no difference at all

4. Every good work, every miracle of grace and every spiritual advancement is a result of the Holy Spirit, who:
   a. lets us know His Name
   b. directs our praise toward the Father or the Son
   c. never draws attention to Himself
   d. both b & c

5. What consumes the Holy Spirit's thoughts?
   a. getting to go home during the Rapture
   b. whether we are going to allow Him to do a miracle
   c. seeing Jesus glorified and the Father's will accomplished on earth
   d. doing the right thing

6. The Holy Spirit accomplishes the work of the Godhead:
   a. yet He never revealed His personal name
   b. for us to celebrate
   c. so we know who's in charge
   d. to announce the compound names of the Holy Spirit

7. The God-pattern we see in the Holy Spirit that leads us to spiritual rest and maturity is:
   a. seeking reward
   b. complete obedience
   c. perfect humility
   d. both b & c

8. When Pastor Francis uses the phrase "to delight in hiddenness," it means:
   a. directing all praise toward Christ and God the Father
   b. hiding in our prayer closet
   c. abandoning recognition for our service
   d. both a & c

ANSWER KEY TO THIS SESSION'S
SELF TEST QUESTIONS:

CHAPTER ELEVEN. Surrender of the Vision-
Keeper
1.b, 2.d, 3.d, 4.b, 5.d, 6.c, 7.d, 8.d.
CHAPTER TWELVE. To Delight in Hiddenness
1.a, 2.b, 3.a, 4.d, 5.c, 6.a, 7.d, 8.d.

ONLINE RESOURCES FOR
IN CHRIST'S IMAGE TRAINING

ONLINE SCHOOL INFORMATION

ICIT online school was established to empower individuals seeking greater conformity to Christ. Students from around the world register online and then receive two written messages each week via email. They also receive a set of 39 audio teachings (on 24 CDs or cassettes), which complement the written messages and add to the training. Students are then tested every six weeks and receive a cumulative grade at the end of six months; they also receive Level I certification from In Christ's Image Training.

The text materials used by our online school have been upgraded and reproduced into these four Level I manuals. If you are interested in continuing your studies, or if you desire certification through *In Christ's Image Training,* you will need to purchase and study the audio messages that accompany these manuals (see the following resource pages). You will then need to take a separate exam that will confirm to us that you have understood the training materials and are, indeed, pursuing the character of Christ.

For more information about current prices, special offers and the benefits of *In Christ's Image Training,* visit our web site at www.ICITC.org. No one will be refused training due to lack of funds.

In Christ's Image Training
Curriculum Package Options

Level I Basic Training
(using Arrow Publications materials)
In Basic Training, the student/group studies at their own pace.

Full course: manuals and audio messages	$172.00
Manuals only (four books: Christlikeness, Humility, Prayer, Unity)	$52.00
Audio only (24 CDs or tapes)	$120.00

Materials available: Four manuals and 39 audio messages
(see back of Unity book for session and audio titles)

Note: If you purchased this Basic Training package, you can still later enroll in the online school. To officially complete Level I and receive ICIT certification, you must enroll in our online school and successfully pass the final exam, after studying all manuals and audio teachings. Tuition cost for completion of Level I is $68.00. Visit www.ICITC.org for Level II tuition fees.

Level I Premium Package
(Enrollment in *ICIT* Online School)

When enrolled in ICIT Level I Online School, the commitment is for six months of training via weekly email lessons. Testing will be done every six weeks, following the completion of each track (Christlikeness, Humility, Prayer, Unity).

Individual Tuition	$240.00
Married Couple	$350.00
Group rate (per person, in group of six or more)	$85.00

Materials provided:
- Sessions introduced through weekly email
- 39 audio messages on 24 CDs or tapes (included in tuition)

Benefits of Enrollment in *ICIT* Level I Online School:
- Interaction with *ICIT* school and other *ICIT* students
- Invitation to annual On-site Impartation Seminar
- Certification with *In Christ's Image Training*
- Diploma signed by Francis Frangipane
- Opportunity to advance to Level II training
- Opportunity to advance to Level III training
- Opportunity to join Association of Pastors, Leaders, and Intercessors

For more information visit www.ICITC.org.

NOTE:As an ICIT Level I online student, you are entitled to purchase one set of study manuals at a 50% discount, $26.00, from Arrow Publications.

ICIT Member Churches/Organizations

ICIT member churches/organizations may receive substantial discounts or other benefits for your church or organization when you purchase ICIT materials through Arrow Publications. For the most current offers and news, visit www.ICITC.org.

BOOKS BY FRANCIS FRANGIPANE

CALL FOR QUANTITY DISCOUNTS ON 10+ BOOKS!

IT'S TIME TO END CHURCH SPLITS

Not only is the deception surrounding splits exposed, but we are brought to a place of healing where we can possess the "unoffendable" heart of Jesus Christ.

#FF1-026   retail $10.50   our price $10.00

THE DAYS OF HIS PRESENCE

Published by Kingdom Publishing.

As the day of the Lord draws near, though darkness covers the earth, the outraying of Christ's Presence shall arise and appear upon His people!

#FF2-021   retail $11.00   our price $9.00

THE STRONGHOLD OF GOD

(formerly The Place of Immunity)

Published by Creation House.

A road map into the shelter of the Most High. The atmosphere of thanksgiving, praise, faith and love are places of immunity for God's servant.

#FF2-009   retail $13.00   our price $10.00

THE POWER OF COVENANT PRAYER

(formerly The Divine Antidote)

Published by Creation House.

Takes the reader to a position of victory over witchcraft and curses. A must for those serious about attaining Christlikeness.

#FF2-010   retail $10.00   our price $9.00

THE POWER OF ONE CHRISTLIKE LIFE

Published by Whitaker House.

The prayer of a Christlike intercessor is the most powerful force in the universe, delaying God's wrath until He pours out His mercy.

#FF1-025   retail $11.00   our price $10.00

THE THREE BATTLEGROUNDS

An in-depth view of three arenas of spiritual warfare: the mind, the church and the heavenly places.   #FF1-001   our price $9.00

#FF1-022 **hardcover**   our price $14.75

HOLINESS, TRUTH AND THE PRESENCE OF GOD

A penetrating study of the human heart and how God prepares it for His glory. This classic devotional has become a favorite of teachers, students and all who are seeking to know the fullness of God's heart.

#FF1-002   our price $9.00

THE HOUSE OF THE LORD

Published by Creation House.

Pleads God's case for a Christlike church as the only hope for our cities. It takes a citywide church to win the citywide war.

#FF1-004   retail $10.00   our price $9.00

DISCIPLESHIP TRAINING BOOKLETS

$3.95 EACH (10+ AT 40%, 100+ AT 50% DISCOUNT)

COMPILED/FORMATTED FOR GROUP STUDY BY FRANCIS FRANGIPANE

A TIME TO SEEK GOD   #FF1-020 $3.95

DISCERNING OF SPIRITS BESTSELLER!   #FF1-018 $3.95

THE JEZEBEL SPIRIT BESTSELLER!   #FF1-019 $3.95

EXPOSING THE ACCUSER OF THE
     BRETHREN BESTSELLER!   #FF1-017 $3.95

PREVAILING PRAYER   #FF1-011 $3.95

REPAIRERS OF THE BREACH   #FF1-013 $3.95

DELIVERANCE FROM PMS   #DF1-002 $3.95

OVERCOMING FEAR!   #DF1-003 $3.95
       BY DENISE FRANGIPANE

TAPE ALBUMS

TAPE OF THE MONTH ANNUAL SUBSCRIPTION IS $54.50 (INCLUDING S&H)

TO KNOW GOD   #1FF5-032   4 tapes $20.00

IN HOLY FEAR   #1FF5-036   5 tapes $25.00

PRAYER WARRIOR   #1FF5-034   3 tapes $15.00

ON THE ARMS OF OUR BELOVED
       #1FF5-037   5 tapes $25.00

RECOMMENDED READING AND SELECTED CLASSICS

EVANGELISM BY FIRE
   by Reinhard Bonnke   #RB1-001   retail $15.00

INTERCESSORY PRAYER
   by Dutch Sheets   #DS1-001   retail $12.99

THE PROPHETIC MINISTRY
   by Rick Joyner   #RJ1-001   retail $12.99

YES, LORD! (LEARNING COVENANT THROUGH
MARRIAGE) by Sherry Thornton   #ST1-001   retail $12.00

FULL LIFE IN CHRIST (formerly LIKE CHRIST)
   by Andrew Murray   #AM1-001   retail $10.99

WAITING ON GOD
   by Andrew Murray   #AM1-002   retail $6.99

CHANGED INTO HIS LIKENESS
   by Watchman Nee   #WN1-001   retail $6.99

SIT, WALK, STAND
   by Watchman Nee   #WN1-002   retail $4.99

THE GREAT DIVORCE
   by C.S. Lewis   #CSL1-001   retail $9.95

PRACTICE OF THE PRESENCE OF GOD
   by Brother Lawrence   #BL1-001   retail $4.99

CO-PUBLISHED BY ARROW PUBLICATIONS

BREAKING CHRISTIAN CURSES: FINDING
   FREEDOM FROM DESTRUCTIVE PRAYERS
       #DC1-001   retail $15.00

YOU CAN ALL PROPHESY   #DC1-002   retail $10.00

THE NEXT 100 YEARS   #DC1-003   retail $12.00

       BY DENNIS CRAMER

JOURNAL OF THE UNKNOWN PROPHET
   by Wendy Alec   #WA1-001   retail $18.00   our price $16.00

THE BIRTH OF YOUR DESTINY
   by Victoria Boyson   #VBI1-001   retail $12.95   our price $10.95

FALLING TO HEAVEN
   by Mickey Robinson   #MR1-001   retail $12.00

HELP! I'M STUCK WITH THESE PEOPLE FOR
   THE REST OF ETERNITY!   *New!*
   by Susan Gaddis   #SG1-001   retail $12.00